D0850702

A Practical Guide to Fund-raising in Schools

Government funding for education is limited and schools are increasingly having to raise funds through schemes involving community and commercial support. The OFSTED inspection programme expects schools to produce detailed management plans including how they will find the resources to realise these plans.

This practical guide explains everything that schools need to know about funding, including:

- who to involve in fund-raising;
- where to look for sources of funding;
- how to set and meet fund-raising targets;
- case studies of fund-raising initiatives;
- contact details of useful organisations.

All schools looking to develop commercial and community partnerships should invest in a copy of this guide: the answer to every headteacher's funding prayer.

Paul Morris has substantial experience of financial management in an education setting and runs his own Educational Resource Improvement Consultancy (ERIC).

A Practical Guide to Fund-raising in Schools

Paul Morris

London and New York

First published 2000
by Routledge
11 New Fetter Lane, London EC4P 4EE

Simultaneously published in the USA and Canada
by Routledge
29 West 35th Street, New York, NY 10001

Routledge is an imprint of the Taylor & Francis Group

© 2000 Paul Morris

Typeset in Palatino by Taylor & Francis Books Ltd
Printed and bound in Great Britain by Clays Ltd, St Ives plc

British Library Cataloguing in Publication Data
A catalogue record for this book is available from the British
Library

Library of Congress Cataloging in Publication Data
Morris, Paul
    A practical guide to fund-raising in schools/Paul Morris.
    p. cm.
    Includes bibliographical references and index.
    1. Educational fund raising – Great Britain – Handbooks,
    manuals, etc. 2. Schools – Great Britain – Finance –
    Handbooks, manuals, etc. 3. Grants-in-aid – Great Britain –
    Directories. I. Title.
    LC245.G7 .M67 2000   99-087277

ISBN 0–415–22957–X

Contents

Foreword

In most countries, there is an ever widening gap between the cost of running schools and the level of funding available from governments. Though social expectations of schools continue to rise, there is a reluctance on the part of most taxpayers to pay any more for education. These are the elements of the financial crisis now facing many of our schools.

To survive, we in education must adopt new strategies, become more commercial in outlook and show greater inventiveness in the way we operate. We need to change to flexible, quick response organisations which can pick up windfalls or adjust to new situations at a speed not normally associated with schools. Sitting back and blaming the system will not put more computers in our classrooms, and we must contemplate a compete culture change. Without doubt the future will about making more from less.

This new funding guide is a useful introduction to the 'self-help' world which schools now inhabit and gives many practical tips.

Sir Bob Salisbury
Headteacher, Garibaldi School
Mansfield

Abbreviations

ABSA	Association for Business Sponsorship of the Arts
A4E	Arts for Everyone
AMP	Asset Management Plan
BITC	Business in the Community
CSV	Community Service Volunteers
DfEE	Department for Education and Employment
DTI	Department for Trade and Industry
EBP	Education–Business Partnership
ICT	Information and Communication Technology
LEA	Local Education Authority
LEC	Local Enterprise Company (Scotland only)
LGA	Local Government Association
LMS	Local Management of Schools
NDS	New Deal for Schools
NFER	National Federation for Education Research
NOF	New Opportunities Fund
OFSTED	Office for Standards in Education
PFI	Private Finance Initiative
PPP	Public Private Partnership
PSA	Parents Staff Association
PTA	Parent Teacher Association
SMEs	Small and Medium-sized Enterprises
SWOT	Strengths, Weaknesses, Opportunities and Threats
TC	Technology College
TEC	Training and Enterprise Council
TVEI	Technical and Vocational Education Initiative

Introduction
Finding your inspiration

In the late 1980s, a headteacher, freshly appointed at a state secondary school in the East Midlands, stood back to take stock of his fresh challenge and the environment in which the school existed. The local area had suffered economic deprivation. Until recently, employment had come from long-established industries such as coal-mining and textiles, and new employment opportunities were slow to develop.

The main results of his stock-taking can be summarised as follows:

- the school was in the bottom six schools in its LEA for GCSE results;
- the annual buildings repair bill at the school was in excess of £40,000;
- every year fifty intake students were opting for other local secondary schools;
- there were only eight students in the school's sixth form;
- staff morale was low.

He also knew that, while the standard education funding sources were either contracting or remaining at the same levels, the funding levels required to achieve the aims and objectives at the school were steadily rising. He had to respond to this dilemma. Standing still or going backwards were not options that he was willing to consider.

His response was to develop a programme of initiatives, in both the pastoral and curricular areas of his school, which would encourage the introduction of partnerships between the school and commerce.

These local and national partnerships enabled the school to take advantage of funding opportunities, from both UK trusts and European funding initiatives, which brought about the following changes:

- GCSE results have improved over 300 per cent in a four-year period;
- vandalism and truancy have been greatly reduced;
- the school is now oversubscribed year on year;
- there are now over 130 members of the sixth form;
- staff morale is excellent, with Heads of Curriculum areas developing their own resourcefulness to bring opportunities to pupils, often supported by commercial and educational partners.

This school does exist. The headteacher is Sir Bob Salisbury. The school is the Garibaldi School, Mansfield, Nottinghamshire, and it featured as one of the case studies in Sir John Harvey-Jones's series on BBC2 *The Trouble-shooter Returns*.

Among the visitors to the school have been HRH Prince Charles and David Blunkett (then Shadow Secretary of State for Education), together with a stream of headteachers, all keen to find the source of the miracles performed at this normal state secondary school.

This may not be the first time that you have heard of such initiatives, but maybe you thought that these entrepreneurial and innovative organisations were the exception rather than the rule.

However, you may be surprised to find that there are schools in your local area who have achieved similar success, and that there are various other examples across the country of schools developing partnerships with community groups and businesses in order to take advantage of funding opportunities.

Opportunities for alternative sources of funding in education have certainly been on the increase in recent years. With the correct approach, all schools can utilise these opportunities to the benefit of their pupils and their local community.

So, can your school join this number of enriched education

centres? Perhaps the first step is to decide whether the advice in this guide can be used in your school.

Why this guide is needed

Scarcity of funds

Schools, particularly those in the state sector, have found that funding available from the customary sources has become scarcer. In real terms, the value of this funding has fallen without keeping pace with either salary increases or inflation. It is now recognised that reliance on the state for full educational funding is no longer valid and that alternative strategies need to be sought.

There can be few headteachers who lie awake, night after night, worrying how to spend the excess funds available to their school. More realistic is insomnia brought on because there are too many calls on the scarce funding available.

More development planning

There has been a rise in the importance attached to development planning in schools. As a management tool, this concept has been in evidence for some time in education, but recent bodies such as TVEI and OFSTED have significantly raised its prominence.

Very few school inspections in the past few years have not resulted in each school formulating a development plan, together with an action plan outlining the delivery of the plan's aims and objectives. All well and good, until schools look at the availability of resources required to implement these plans. It is in this area that the more resourceful schools have developed programmes and initiatives designed to deliver their action plans with innovative approaches to access funding. Often such programmes have involved community and commercial support, while also developing project management skills.

Changes in school management

There has been a substantial shift in the past decade regarding how schools are managed, whether in specific curriculum areas, across the curriculum (e.g. ICT), or on whole-school issues. This has meant that financial management has become an aspect of the day-to-day work of heads of departments, senior teachers, school managers and governors. Therefore, the availability (or scarcity) of resources has, in many instances, become a local rather than a central issue.

However, it is not simply a matter of sending young Oliver up to the DfEE or the LEA to ask 'Can I have some more, please, Sir?' There is a need for schools to offer more focused programmes, with more deserving aims, and a professional approach, in order to have a better chance of winning the funding they seek.

A national shift in approach

The need to develop alternative strategies for fund-raising in education has become an issue which is now receiving widespread attention throughout the world of education.

This need is not only being actively encouraged by those directly involved in delivering the best available service to pupils, but also by those responsible for national education policies.

Initiatives, such as the New Deal for Schools programme, talk of a portion of the funding being a 'local contribution'. Such schemes actively encourage public–private partnership funding.

Similarly, the benefits of resource improvement in education are being recognised as not only a financial investment in the future of schools and colleges, but also having secondary benefits in improving standards, both social and academic, and reducing expenditure in areas such as vandalism and buildings maintenance.

Who is this guide for?

School staff

This guide is primarily aimed at both teaching and support staff, school management teams and governors in all schools, whether primary or secondary, state-funded or voluntary-aided, foundation or independent.

You could be interested in this because of the following reasons:

- you have a duty to deliver efficient, economic and effective financial management in your school;
- you have recognised that a lack of funding is preventing your school from achieving its objectives;
- you have responsibilities in your school for the management and delivery of a specific curriculum area;
- you have been allocated extra responsibilities for community development or out-of-school activities;
- your teaching career is in a developmental phase, and you are wondering how to advance the management strategies in your school;
- you have identified a specific resource need either in a specialised field or as a whole-school issue.

In all these instances, the aim is that this guide will provide you with ideas and approaches which can make your fund-raising strategy successful.

Included are case studies of successful schools who have recognised that resource improvement programmes are not only about accessing important sources of funding. They also provide an exercise in building on the existing strengths and assets of the organisation, especially the human resource potential of teachers, managers and support staff.

More and more, good practitioners in this field are coming to the fore, sharing their experience with other schools so that the communal learning curve is less steep.

In the case studies in this guide, commentators readily admit the lessons they have learnt and are happy to pass on these tips to newcomers.

Education administrators

The guide is also very relevant for education administrators, whether in local government or with other educational bodies, who consider resource improvement programmes as a means of raising standards.

Recent funding initiatives have placed Local Education Authorities (LEAs) in the role of facilitators. In certain instances, LEA officers are being asked to prioritise bids for funding in schemes, and to decide which should be put forward. This means that the partnership between individual school managers and LEA officers has become even more important. It is now essential that all LEA officers understand the individual strengths, requirements and aims of all the schools in their area. They also need to be able to communicate the LEA's wider educational resource strategy to these schools.

Those in local government have to be aware of the funding opportunities available, and be prepared to encourage schools to consider these possibilities.

How can this guide be of use?

Where your aims and objectives are thwarted by lack of funding and resources, this guide can offer you solutions, ideas and direction to overcome these problems. This is done by providing the following:

- examples of proactive approaches that have been successful in other schools;
- details of trusts, companies and other organisations who support education;
- advice from practitioners on the steps to take in resource project development;
- tips on identifying contacts, making approaches and presenting projects and proposals positively and creatively.

How is the guide set out?

The guide takes the form of a journey. Any project has a start and a destination and fund-raising is no different. The stages taken to reach your chosen destination are just as important. Within the Introduction, it is hoped that you can grasp the inspiration to set out on this fund-raising journey.

Chapter 1 helps you to see why you need to make this journey; identifying your reasons for being interested in fund-raising for your school; and then using school development planning as a launch pad to identify your areas of resource needs.

Chapter 2 is about recognising your destination and the right direction to take. Here you can design your own school's fund-raising strategy, based on your recognised strengths, making the most of the opportunities available to your school.

Chapter 3 gives advice on entering into local partnerships either with statutory bodies, commercial enterprises, grant-awarding bodies, community groups or other organisations with similar aims – finding companions to keep you company on your journey.

On your fund-raising journey, there are places to visit and sights to see. In Chapter 4 you can discover the substantial number of funding agencies, from government bodies to trusts to corporate funding, that exist to provide support for many educational issues.

All expeditions need to have a solid home base to provide support and encouragement. In Chapter 5 we look at the internal funding options available to schools. Is there still a role for car-boot sales and school fêtes? Can your creativity breathe new life into these traditional fund-raising exercises?

Throughout the journey, introductions will need to be made and support gained. Chapter 6 details how to initiate contact with possible funding partners; how to keep relationships with these organisations on an even keel, and what to do to increase your chances of success with grant-making or funding organisations.

Successful journeys rely on strong and positive teamwork. Chapter 7 explores the pros and cons of the team approach; how to prevent your team becoming a committee, and getting the most out of team meetings.

Chapter 8 helps you to make the most of your fund-raising project through effective management, with recommended stages and routines from good practitioners – ultimately reaching your destination.

Finally, Chapter 9 looks at how to develop ongoing strategies, keeping your options open and funds flowing – planning the next campaign.

Rising to the challenge

This guide does not offer any ready-made formulas to guarantee funds, but it can help you to develop fund-raising strategies with a greater chance of success. There can be little doubt that obtaining funding from external sources is not a simple task. You need to have a clear focus and be innovative and creative in the ways in which fund-raising schemes are conceived.

Grant-making bodies are receiving an ever-increasing number of enquiries for their finite funds. So your school needs approaches and initiatives which stand head and shoulders above the rest.

Consider how a personal approach to a bank manager for a loan, or a commercial prospect is viewed by an investment agency. Is it more likely to succeed if the funding request has a clear purpose and is professionally formulated?

If you can also show that the results of these increased funds will lead to the desired outcome, in both educational and community areas, then your chances of success will also increase.

This guide will assist you to let your school join the ever-increasing number who have introduced resource improvement programmes as part of their development planning process.

The case studies cover a wide range of schools whose only common trait has been a desire to do something positive regarding the scarcity of funding in education, rather than just accept the situation. These schools are finding that the enhanced resources result in improved educational standards, more job satisfaction for teachers, and a better relationship with organisations outside the boundaries of the school.

Chapter 1

Why do you need to make a fund-raising journey?

One of the most difficult aspects of any initiative, scheme or project is knowing where to start. This is clearly a view shared by the headteacher of a state secondary school in Dudley, currently the second most successful school to be awarded National Lottery funds – over £4 million in 1997 – who commented that if she was asked to start the bid process over again, she would tackle it in a completely different manner.

Experience, once gained, can be a wonderful asset and hindsight is always 20/20, but how should you start the process of fund-raising in your school? One method is to use a well-known problem-solving technique known as the five Ws and H:

- WHO? – this relates to your school, but it could also involve local community groups with similar aims;
- WHERE? – this normally relates to a project on your school site;

  WHEN? – with funding issues this is always as soon as possible, but later in this guide you will see how, by using stages and milestones, the 'WHEN' can become well defined;

  WHY? and WHAT? – these questions may relate to a single problem to be resolved, or cover a number of goals, so it might be prudent to look first at some of the reasons for fund-raising at your school;

  HOW? – this relates to the process that you would undertake to achieve your fund-raising goals.

These questions may not always occur in the same order but they all need answers. Some of them may be relatively simple to answer in your school.

Why are you interested in fund-raising for your school and in what areas?

Maybe you are in charge of a curriculum area in your school. Having explored the possibilities of delivering your subject in a more interesting and positive manner, you have identified a need for investment over and above your standard annual departmental budget.

Or you may be a parent-governor who has seen little or no investment in the school buildings for a number of years. You are acutely aware of the impact this has on staff morale, vandalism and admission numbers.

Or you may be aware that the annual repair bill is always in excess of the allowed budget and so vital funding for curriculum areas is swallowed up by building maintenance work.

You may also be aware of the lack of important resources for both young people and community groups in the local environment of your school.

Or as headteacher, you are aware that there are specialities and strengths in your school which need to be encouraged and developed, but this can only be done with extra funding.

Perhaps you are a governor appointed by the LEA and from your contacts you know that there are mutually beneficial opportunities for links with organisations, possibly businesses or voluntary groups, in your local community.

Or as a teacher, you may have become aware of the many opportunities for pupils to visit theatres, galleries, events and exhibitions – initiatives which have been set up especially for schools. Sadly, there never seems to be enough funding available to cover such trips and so these opportunities go begging – unless you ask the parents to pay.

You could be a senior teacher in charge of the pastoral aspects of pupil development. Your work is constantly thwarted by low morale from the teaching staff and a mediocre environment which does nothing to encourage the pupils to take pride in their school.

As a Deputy Head in charge of admissions you have seen a constant stream of prospective pupils attend your Open Day only to find that they have selected other local schools in the following September.

Or simply you have been delegated the task of finding extra funds for your school and you don't know where to start.

Whether you are a governor, teacher, manager or parent, you may recognise some of these scenarios in your school. They are all realistic, often connected and never unique.

You may find that you have different reasons for seeking funds for your school, but in recognising your fund-raising needs you have taken the first step in the long journey towards meeting these needs.

So now that you have a clearer picture of why you need to raise funds for your school, the next stage is to identify the steps that can be of use in getting started on your fund-raising strategy. Here the motto is 'Do not re-invent the wheel'. The first step has already been taken for you and exists in the form of a document that most schools have become familiar with in the past few years – the school development plan.

Why start with the school development plan?

You should begin here because schools have been strongly encouraged to develop this form of strategic planning, especially following school inspections. Most schools have gone through an OFSTED inspection at least once over the past five years and have become accustomed to devising action plans that will attend to the key issues raised in those inspections.

It is, like most management tools, not a new concept, but in this particular instance it has a great deal of value in that it affords each school the opportunity to state its aims and objectives clearly.

It has also created a planning process which assists in identifying how these goals can be achieved, and advocates methods of assessment which will monitor progress regarding the delivery of action plans, both for the school as a whole and in individual curriculum areas.

Schools have also been encouraged to develop a 'mission statement' which sums up their educational goals in a concise manner. This statement is devised by consultation with all stakeholders – pupils, teachers, managers, governors and parents – and this ownership provides you with a template for the ethos of your school.

Individual areas of growth

The development plan is often separated into the areas of growth which are needed in order that the school can progress, e.g. pupil development; academic achievement; staff development; image; and quality of environment.

Each of these sections is supported by individual plans from each curriculum area in the school. Thus the overall plan is constructed and developed in both directions – bottom up from the curriculum departments, and top down from the determining mission statement. This style of planning encourages schools to communicate their aims and objectives to all parties – parents, staff, pupils, governors, managers and the community in which it exists.

This manifesto now exists in each school. It can be used to identify the areas where funding or resources are required. It is the blueprint from which to develop fund-raising strategies.

Using SWOT analysis

School development planning is often extremely useful in identifying the areas of expertise in your school. This can also be done by carrying out an organisational SWOT analysis, to identify the Strengths, Weaknesses, Opportunities and Threats that exist in your school.

In a SWOT analysis carried out in a LEA secondary school in Hampshire in 1995, the following features were identified.

Strengths

First, this school had consistently good exam results in Arts and Science subjects. Unsurprisingly, teachers, pupils and parents often view academic success as the only measurement of a school's strength. Sometimes these can be in a specific subject where exam results are constantly high and the popularity of the subject is reflected in pupil choice and parental support. However, schools have other important strengths.

Second, a recent inspection had commented on the caring attitude of all staff. It is sometimes overlooked that the professionalism of the staff and their length of service are a strong indication of the commitment and proficiency available to pupils – again, a major strength.

Third, another strength identified reflected the demographics of the area in which the school was located. While situated in a residential area, with a high proportion of parents having professional occupations, the school is close to the local town centre, as well as many established factories and businesses. Similarly, the ease of access with regard to the local transportation was seen as a strength.

Finally, the school's possession of large and pleasant playing fields was advantageous both from the educational and community points of view.

Weaknesses

First, the main weakness related to the unattractive buildings at the school, and the lack of repairs and maintenance over several decades.

Second, a fragmented management structure with responsibilities split between the school's management team, the governing body and the LEA, was also cited as a weakness.

Opportunities

Only limited opportunities were identified. First, the future of the school appeared more secure as a major new housing development was forecast in the catchment area.

Second, opportunities to specialise existed, either as a centre of excellence in a particular curricular area, or as an educational centre for students of all ages. However these could only be grasped once further funding or management resources were made available.

Finally, the opportunity of developing community links with local sporting associations was already being investigated.

Threats

First, in the school's LEA, certain secondary schools were heavily under-subscribed and performing poorly. This situation had occurred a decade earlier, resulting in the restructuring of five secondary schools down to four.

Also, the school was close to West Sussex, where education was perceived as being better funded, more disciplined and with higher than average exam results.

Finally, the area has a long-standing tradition of private education which tended to recruit the more able pupils. Local private schools were set to expand in spite of the effect of recent economic recession on their intake.

All these SWOT factors need to be taken into account by this school both when designing a strategy to attract parents and pupils to the school, and to empower managers at the school to attract the best teaching staff. They are also fundamental when deciding the best approach to fund-raising.

Like most processes, the SWOT learning curve is steep to start with but, given time, the process becomes part of the organisational fabric. The inevitable resistance to new concepts decreases, especially as teachers, governors and parents begin to recognise the benefits – clarity of focus, improved teamwork and celebrating success.

Case study

At a High School in Yorkshire, development planning has been combined with SWOT analysis to provide an approach to fund-raising which is reaping major dividends. The head-teacher describes this approach as a 'partnership with the community' with its starting point being a clear guiding philosophy arising from the school development plan, in which the following statement appears: 'Our commitment to developing partnership opportunities with outside agencies and institutions, for the benefit of our students, drives much of our planning.'

The school now holds an annual planning process including reviews of departmental, examination and middle management performance. Teachers and students are equally involved in these reviews.

Coupled with this process, the school holds SWOT sessions, again involving teachers and students but, vitally in this instance, also involving members of the local business community and school governors.

The headteacher believes that, since they have asked the school's customers what their expectations were of the services provided, the school has been making better and more informed decisions when it comes to meeting the local community needs.

Moreover, the school publishes its commitment to the local community, and has come to regard wide-ranging consultation with local interests as a vital part of developing its fund-raising strategy.

As a result, a multitude of fund-raising opportunities have arisen. The school's £38,000 budget deficit has been turned into a £50,000 surplus. Among the many successes is £5,000 donated by a local factory after only twenty minutes discussion with their sales team, and £15,000 received in reply to a single letter.

Significantly, partnership with the community has also brought with it the benefits of decreasing vandalism and truancy, and improvements in exam performance.

How will the school development plan help me get started?

The groundwork has already been done

The aims and objectives of each school have been well thought through in each plan, with input from many of the school's stakeholders – teachers, parents, governors, students and managers. It is this process that provides you with a clear focus of where your school wishes to go as an organisation, and what it wishes to achieve.

Similarly, in each of your curriculum areas, Heads of Departments have formulated how to deliver their plans, and in each instance they are encouraged to cost out new schemes so that their individual resource needs are clearly stated. Thus, it is only a matter of looking at your development plan to put together a list of your resource needs, whether on a whole-school basis or for individual subjects.

Development planning is essential

The process of development planning is one of great professionalism. It involves in-depth examination, questioning and analysis of not only the needs of your school, but also its current strengths and advantages.

This evaluative approach is crucial to all fund-raising schemes. Certainly it is an absolute requirement in bidding for National Lottery funding, and other grant-awarding bodies will be impressed by your school's in-depth consideration of the issues you wish to address.

Similarly, initiatives such as the Specialist Schools Programme require schools to submit a development plan detailing how they will progress as centres of excellence in their chosen curriculum strength. Therefore, the manner in which the data identifying the specific resources needed is presented can have a critical influence on the success of your fund-raising schemes.

Development planning can help you decide on your destination

Your development plan not only can act as a guide but can also provide a series of destinations. The detailed resource needs can provide both small-scale and major initiatives for fund-raising.

A word of warning: many experienced fund-raisers wish they had cut their teeth on a small project, and used its success to develop larger schemes. Often smaller schemes can introduce the school to the whole process of community involvement, project management and partnership funding on a manageable scale.

There have been many schools where the fear of trying to raise thousands of pounds for a capital project, involving substantial matched funding, has resulted in projects being ditched at the first sign of difficulty.

Many success stories abound with dead ends, hurdles and disappointments, but perseverance has enabled the rewards to be quite astounding. The aforementioned school from Dudley had to re-submit their National Lottery bid twice before they gained their awards.

It improves the manner in which the outside world perceives resource management in schools

In fact, this fourth aspect is allied to that of professionalism in that the tone of your school development plan can show your local community how innovative and entrepreneurial your school can be.

Many fund-raising schemes currently involve partnerships with organisations in both the public and private sectors. In all these instances, the higher the organisational integrity of your school, the more likely it is that the fund-raising outcomes will be successful.

Good fund-raising practitioners stress that the school's approach should always be professional and businesslike, matched with large doses of creativity and lateral thinking.

Case study

A secondary school in Hertfordshire is a good example showing how the combination of vision, determination, and luck played a vital role in securing a grant in excess of £100,000. The school had recognised that one of its strengths lay in the skills and experience that they had developed in teaching modern languages – a strength that could help in their aim of becoming a Language College, as part of the DfEE's Specialist Schools Programme.

The DfEE guidelines for this initiative were used as a blueprint for their fund-raising drive. Partners had to be found to provide the matched funding of £100,000 required for this initiative, and the school's approach to the task was both methodical and professional.

All the local medium-sized and large businesses were contacted to find out where language skills were required, and personal contact was made with those who expressed a common interest.

A brochure was produced that concisely outlined their goal of becoming a Language College, offering full details of staff expertise and academic successes, particularly current examination results in modern languages. The support already gained from their local MP was also stressed. This impressed many local organisations but this interest was not initially matched with offers of funding support. Not, that is, without a somewhat fortuitous circumstance.

A major supermarket company, whose headquarters are based nearby, were undertaking international expansion and their needs – language training for their key staff – could be met by supporting this scheme. This company offered to become the major private sector sponsor in this project, with other companies then following suit.

The headteacher is convinced that it was his school's professional approach that attracted this major funding support. With this funding on board they were able to obtain the approval of the DfEE for their application to become a Language College.

He also admits that this success was also due to being in the right place at the right time, with the right scheme. Without his vision and determination, however, perhaps the opportunities in the local community would never have been discovered.

Having a member of the fund-raising team who has the knack of making happy and unexpected discoveries by accident is a welcome bonus to any school's fund-raising strategy!

Chapter 2

What is your fund-raising destination and what direction do you need to take?

Therefore, having resolved that the school development plan is to be your starting point, the next step is to design a fund-raising strategy or strategies for your school.

In this chapter, the guide will seek to clarify the following:

- what should be in your fund-raising strategy;
- who formulates the strategy;
- what assistance is available to help you plan your strategy.

It may be that you need different strategies for each fund-raising scheme. For example, a large-scale capital programme, possibly involving National Lottery funding, will require a different approach from a fund-raising exercise to support local out-of-school activities.

Clarification can be found by considering the various elements that will be crucial to your fund-raising strategy, namely:

- the aims of your strategy;
- setting targets and milestones;
- the personnel involved;
- the resources needed;
- the audience for your strategy;
- who can help you with your strategy.

The strategy's aims

Here we look at the goals that your strategy wishes to achieve and some of the existing factors which can assist in bringing success. Obviously, the aims of your strategy will be defined by your fund-raising focus. For example, if your focus is connected with a particular curricular area, then your strategy should involve contacting organisations who have a known interest in that subject. You should also build on the strengths that you have already identified in this particular subject area.

However, if the focus has a broad appeal or a whole school aspect, you may need to clearly define your strategy in order to progress from this somewhat nebulous position. Here again, the five Ws and H concept can be of assistance:

- WHO will be responsible for the strategy and WHO can deliver the strategy?
- WHY are the funds required?
- WHAT level of funding is required?
- WHEN are the funds to be raised by?
- WHERE are the funds to be spent?
- HOW will the funding aims be achieved?

You may not yet have absolute answers to all these questions or be able to define each item of resource or each person who will be involved, but by considering these aspects now you can provide both clarity and purpose which will stand you in good stead. In short, the aims of your strategy need to be clear, concise and easily understood by all those involved. However, there are certain factors already in existence that can assist in bringing success to your strategy.

Does it fit in with the culture of your school?

The most successful projects have been those which were in keeping with the ethos of the organisation. If your school is proactive and creative in its approach on a general basis, then it is likely to be so when it comes to managing a fund-raising scheme.

Similarly, if your school is cautious but purposeful, then

projects run from within the school are likely to have similar qualities. This is not to say that one approach is better than the other but your school needs to be aware of its characteristic style and be at ease with this especially when considering how possible project partners will react.

Being aware of the style of your school is important. It can be tremendously demanding to try to change the culture of your school, rather than going with the flow.

Is the strategy starting from a position of strength?

Here your development plan should come into its own in that the focus of your fund-raising programme will come from areas where expertise or achievement is already evident in your school. Schools will usually approach the concept of becoming a centre of excellence in a specific curriculum area if their results in that area have been a beacon of success in recent years and the staff involved are fully in favour of this development.

Similarly, if your school excels in sport, maybe champions in many disciplines, then it is more likely to attract support from local community sports organisations.

Are there areas of common purpose within the local community?

Have you identified a local need in the community which can be matched with strengths within the school? Are there any ideas from local groups which correspond with those of the staff, pupils and parents at the school?

These areas of common need are vital from the outset, rather than being identified further down the fund-raising trail. Similarly, areas of possible conflict should be quickly recognised. You will avoid wasting a great deal of time and effort in later stages of your project if you do so.

Case study

A Hampshire town had an excellent Arts Centre. Indeed, it had become so popular with touring companies, concerts and exhibitions that there was little opportunity for local performing arts groups to use the facilities for rehearsals and meetings.

When a nearby school was considering an initiative to improve their Arts facilities – based on their impressive record in performing arts examination results – they contacted the Arts Centre, and began to realise that their initiative could provide the missing rehearsal facilities.

The school was then able to go ahead with the knowledge that local support would be available and that expertise could be gained from the personnel in the Arts Centre built on their own successful growth.

Is your strategy realisable?

This may seem obvious but there are always numerous unanswered questions at the start of a project, such as:

- will partners exist and come forward?
- will the LEA support the project both strategically and financially?
- if you are fund-raising for a new building, could planning permission be a problem?
- can the school manage such a task?
- are there any local bye-laws which would hinder your project?

These are just a few of the issues that will be raised when developing your strategy. Some can be resolved now but you have to be clear that, if there is a major question mark over the scheme, then now is the time to decide whether the strategy can meet its aims, not later.

Targets and milestones

Targets and milestones help you to split up your fund-raising project into manageable segments. These targets and milestones can be any or all of the following.

Levels of funding

Here you may find that a specific level of funding is required before you can move on to other stages. For example, in many matched funding initiatives (and there are plenty around), the percentage that your school needs to have, either available or pledged, may need to be fully documented before your bid can be placed.

Likewise, you may be involved in a scheme that requires a feasibility study to be carried out before major funding can be considered. Here the actual funding of this study, and its constituent elements, may need careful consideration before embarking on the whole project.

Furthermore, identifying the more obvious sources of funding can boost your project. Gaining this support early on in your project can be a major catalyst in finding other supporters and funding opportunities.

Stages in bid procedures

Most grant-awarding bodies will have bid guidelines and procedures. These will detail the stages to follow in order to make your bid. In certain situations this may involve submitting your project details to a third party, e.g. your LEA or the Regional Arts Council.

Similarly, can you identify when trusts, foundations and companies actually allocate funds? If so, then these dates need to be factors in the planning and submission of your fund-raising bids.

In all these instances, the routines should be carefully noted and dates for specific actions duly timetabled. Missing deadlines is both inexcusable and frustrating, and can show a damaging lack of professionalism.

Internally set key markers

There may also be certain pointers in your own school which you need to put into your strategy equation. For example, are you missing key personnel – governors, staff or local councillors – at a time when your project reaches a critical juncture?

Is the climax of your fund-raising initiative at a time when your school is already swamped with either inspections, examinations or school trips?

As we will see, when we consider the resources required for your fund-raising project, timing is not only of the essence but it is also a fundamental factor in internal management issues.

Personnel

Selecting the personnel who will formulate the fund-raising strategy for your school can also be a key issue. Some organisations like to give individual responsibility; others set up a working party immediately.

In either case the question is not how many are involved but are those involved good motivators and communicators? Can they communicate the essence and detail of the strategy to other key personnel?

Some personnel may have already selected themselves – Chairs of Governing Bodies, local councillors or headteachers sometimes do. However, always make room for volunteers, especially those who are keen on your strategy or those who are actively seeking project management experience.

Sometimes those defining the strategy may have been vociferously lobbying for the resources that your fund-raising will provide. Make sure their vocal commitment is matched by their active support.

Who audits your strategy?

To a degree, the personnel who define the strategy need not be responsible for its delivery, but they should remain responsible for monitoring its progress and ensuring that targets are met and milestones reached.

It may often be prudent to appoint one person in your school to have the responsibility of overseeing all fund-raising initiatives.

Persuading the 'doubting Thomas' members of your organisation

Unfortunately, such initiatives always attract a number of doubters, who will pour water on your bonfire. Your mission, should you wish to accept it, is to convince them that there is a very good chance of success and to highlight the benefits, both primary – raising much needed funds, and secondary – improving educational standards.

Your doubters will ask questions such as the following:

- if it was so easy, then why has this not been done before?
- why isn't every school following this course of action, and if they did so, would the grant-making bodies be able to cope?
- why aren't the statutory authorities responsible for all educational funding?

You cannot afford to ignore these questions as you will want as many of your colleagues, whether teachers, support staff, governors or LEA officers, to be as committed to your school's strategy as you are.

If you are honest with yourself, you will be aware that there are bound to be problems to overcome. In no circumstances should you believe that fund-raising is easy or without its fair share of hard work.

There will definitely be setbacks and you will not get every possible partner you approach on board but from the success shown in other projects there is no reason to believe that you will not be able to get enough support to achieve your fund-raising aims.

The best way to convince the 'Yes, but ...' members of your organisation is with honesty and action. Turning malcontents into supporters who become 'Yes, and ...' members of the project can be as rewarding as achieving the fund-raising targets.

There are two main factors already in your favour:

1 As the fund-raising initiative is arising from your school development planning process, it will be well considered and professionally developed.
2 The benefits of the initiative are undeniable, not just the fund-raising, but also the involvement of parties from the school and the local community, the raising of morale and the longer-term benefits of raising educational standards.

These can be very strong arguments.

Resources

Does your school have the resources to deliver the project? There are usually four kinds of resources that the school will need at the start of any fund-raising project – time, motivation, experience and, in certain circumstances, initial finance.

Time

In schools, at present, time is often the most difficult of this quartet to procure, but it is also the most important. Schools seem to be constantly in a state of flux and so time has become as scarce a resource as funding, with managers and teachers alike struggling to adapt within the maelstrom of change.

The availability of time to develop and manage funding initiatives has got to be the area of greatest concern for most schools. The stresses and strains currently felt in education leave little slack, especially the higher up the school you go.

So, can you take on the extra work involved in your fund-raising strategy? Obviously, if the scheme will deliver some of the benefits already outlined, whether primary or secondary, then the investment in time will be worthwhile. There should be little doubt that fund-raising needs both time and commitment to make a success of it.

Some schools are including these responsibilities within their senior management team, others are employing outside fund-raisers, and some are developing a team approach to obtain input from the local community and the school.

In each instance, the school has recognised the need to allocate time and latitude to this purpose. There are plenty of examples where schools have given the fund-raising duties to an already overworked Deputy Head or Head of Department, or they have not allowed time to prepare, discuss and formulate coherent strategies. Unsurprisingly, these examples met with little success.

Motivation

Motivation is allied to your approach and is not as dependent upon internal/external pressures as time. Your school can control the motivational factors within your fund-raising project.

Again, it can be part of your development plan where you have recognised staff whose career path would welcome the opportunity of involvement in, or even leadership of, a fund-raising group.

One school, heavily involved in fund-raising projects, was compared to the Starship *Enterprise*, being one of the first 'to boldly go where no school had gone before'. To continue this analogy, but to move on a generation, the captain on the bridge would bark out the order 'Make it so!' However, he has a crew including telepaths, androids and klingon warriors – do you?

Case study

A Technology teacher at a school in Lancashire has been rewarded for his inventiveness, determination and vision. He initially put forward a proposal to build partnerships with local industry, not only to seek out financial opportunities but also to raise academic achievement, improve public relations and widen the opportunities for student placements.

The proposal was accepted by the headteacher and Chair of Governors, with one reservation – the work would need to be done in the teacher's spare time. Perseverance and resolve, together with a sprinkling of luck, have resulted in the school becoming better off by over £100,000.

The teacher has now been offered the post of full-time development officer for the school, raising a further £120,000 for a computer suite, and writing several articles on fund-raising in schools for educational journals.

Experience

Experience in project management may also be a scarce commodity in your school but do not underestimate your staff. Teachers are not only some of the most flexible employees in the land but they have also developed relevant skills and project management experience within the classroom environment – although they may not realise it!

Teaching demands creativity and innovation, and so they can adapt to managing such initiatives as and when needed. Nor should you overlook the skills of your support staff who may have commercial and administrative skills and experience.

Initial finance

Where some finance is required to 'pump prime' of a project, particularly where feasibility studies are the order of the day, the amount is often only a small proportion of the final fund-raising target.

However, the ability to raise minor sums is often the acid test as to the degree of commitment for your school to take on a larger undertaking. (See Chapter 5.)

Your target audience

Your fund-raising strategy will have to meet the needs of many differing audiences, including:

- the project team;
- all the staff at your school;
- the parents and pupils;
- local community groups;
- local and national commercial organisations;
- your Local Education Authority;

- grant-awarding bodies;
- statutory bodies, e.g. DfEE, Sports Councils.

The need to have a clear focus now becomes more important than ever. All these groups need to understand your purpose simply, clearly and positively if you wish them to support your aims.

So if you ensure that your strategy has been developed in line with your development plan, which already has the 'ownership' and approval of many of these groups, you will assist in bringing this clarity and focus to your fund-raising project and to your audience.

How does your strategy fit in with your school's organisational strengths and opportunities?

For example, a school may realise that its strengths are of a pastoral nature with emphasis on the social development of students. In this instance, the fund-raising strategy could focus on initiatives which develop community awareness, such as the Barclays 'New Futures' Programme – an initiative which provides cash and resources for school/community partnerships involved in social community action projects.

Assistance

As more and more initiatives are undertaken to improve resources in schools, the learning curve for each school is being shortened by the provision of agencies who can provide guidance and advice.

However, one of the lessons being learnt from good practitioners in this field is that of networking, sharing experiences, and creative acquisition – learning from the experience of others and trying not to repeat their mistakes.

Creative acquisition has been an important factor in industry for many years, and there is no reason why education should not follow suit. Again, make sure that in your strategy you are not re-inventing the wheel.

In many fund-raising initiatives and schemes there have been schools who were first to test the water, and many of these are now happy to share their experiences so that you do not have to experience the same disappointments or struggle to overcome the same hurdles. Look out for them in your area.

If these contacts are not obvious, then there are established bodies who can provide such networking for your school. If they cannot help with your problem directly, then they will know someone who has experience of something similar. These include the Technology Colleges Trust and the Youth Sport Trust[1] which have been set up to assist schools interested in the Specialist Schools Programme. On a more general basis, the Education–Business Partnerships together with Business in the Community are welcome sources of advice and assistance.

Never be afraid to ask – it may save you a great deal of time and frustration, and may even result in finding a kindred spirit for your project.

It is not unknown for large corporations to contact agencies such as Training and Enterprise Councils (TECs), to enquire about making sponsorship available for education purposes.

Why do creative and innovative methods in fund-raising projects enhance the chances of success?

This is because, as with any scarce commodity, finding funds and asking people to give their time to a project, paid or otherwise, are becoming more and more difficult as the number of projects increase from schools, clubs and charities.

Accordingly, the number of requests to grant-making bodies has seen a sharp increase and in order to make your bid stand out from the crowd your approach needs to be creative and innovative.

It is only by highlighting the positive benefits to staff, governors, students and parents that you can deliver the vision behind your fund-raising project. If you are unable to light fires in your own camp, how will you fare when you venture to inspire organisations outside the normal education scene?

Even within your LEA you need to gain support from key players, and this will never be managed by tendering a dull and unimaginative fund-raising scheme.

Therefore, methods – such as brain-storming sessions with your colleagues and suggestion boxes from pupils and parents, or competitions for designs or marketing approaches – can give rise to some good, off-the-wall, innovative and interesting ideas.

This may not always be the order of the day in your school, but any one of these ideas can be the factor that makes your scheme stand out – a really vital issue as the number of organisations seeking funding continues to grow.

WIIFM factors – What's In It For Me

This is a term used by Sir Bob Salisbury to describe what each party gains from their involvement in a scheme or initiative.

Case study

As part of their GCSE course work, and in response to the students' enthusiasm, the Head of Technology at a school in Mansfield was keen to take a group to a Robotics exhibition in Glasgow.

After finding out that the cost of the train fare was too high to contemplate, the local airport was approached to see if there were regular flights to Glasgow. The response was in the affirmative, and as flights were usually only half full, the airport said that the school could have the tickets at half price.

The next approach was made to the North Notts TEC, who are often involved in supporting Education–Business Partnerships. They agreed to sponsor the other half, thus in fact covering the whole cost of the flight. Similarly, the exhibition co-ordinators were contacted and also offered free entry.

Finally, The Scotsman newspaper was approached and they agreed to provide taxis to and from Glasgow Airport, and lunch for the group, in exchange for an exclusive article from the school.

All along, the teacher had stressed that this would be an opportunity of a lifetime as, for some of these youngsters, it was the first time that they had flown, and they had shown keen interest and enterprise in this field of engineering.

Not surprisingly, the school in this case study is the Garibaldi School, and the use of WIIFM factors is more than evident:

- there is excellent publicity for the exhibition; an exclusive for the newspaper; and business for the airline;
- both the TEC and the school are meeting their educational aims, and the school is enabling pupils to go to the exhibition without tapping into the school's main budget for the full cost (remembering that supply teachers may have been required to cover the trip).

Sir Bob Salisbury also cites this as a fine example of the essential 'culture change' going on at the school where, if an opportunity becomes blocked financially, other alternatives are sought and found.

Which agencies exist to help your strategy?

Briefly, the following organisations are available to help and they should be the first port of call if seeking advice on your fund-raising strategy:

Local Education Authorities

In many instances, schools will need the full support of their LEA to progress with their fund-raising initiative. LEA representatives bring with them not only experience of similar schemes in other schools but also contacts within local government who can give a wider picture of the use for the benefits that the fund-raising exercise will bring.

Grant-awarding bodies

For example, the staff attached to the six National Lottery grant-awarding bodies can be approached for strategic assistance. Likewise, the various sections of the DfEE have staff who can be approached and may well be able to facilitate your strategic process.

Education–Business Partnerships

In most areas of the UK, these partnerships have been set up to improve links between industry and schools. These organisations are often allied to Business Links, TECs, Chambers of Commerce or Enterprises Agencies – all vital parts of a school's community network.

Local traders associations and business clubs can also be excellent sources of advice and/or assistance.

Libraries

Libraries are often an overlooked source of information and can certainly help with major works on project management, lists of grant-awarding trusts and commercial compendiums.

Relevant local groups

As the possibility of gaining funding may be dependent on the benefits to the local community, therefore representation from, or co-operation with, groups such as Sports Councils, Arts Centres or Community Associations can reap dividends in the future and can provide both advice and experience in developing your fund-raising strategy.

Ignore local groups and societies at your peril. Church organisations often contain records of local trusts – small funding but useful to help get started. Local clubs can provide enthusiasm, contacts and expertise – especially if their aims are similar to yours.

Note

1   For contact details of Technology Colleges and the Youth Sports Trust, see Appendix 1.

Chapter 3

Finding fund-raising companions

Entering into local partnerships

It may be an obvious statement to say that fund-raising is an outgoing exercise, and while it is important to have begun your expedition by deciding where you want to go and what direction to take, it is equally important to consider carefully who your travelling companions may be on this fund-raising journey.

Establish and maintain a contact database for local potential partners in fund-raising

As part of your school's internal audit – carried out during either as part of SWOT analysis sessions, or within your school development planning process – you should be able to recognise organisations in your local environment who could become valuable associates in fund-raising initiatives.

Some of these organisations may be local industries; some may be businesses who have had a local presence for many years; or some may be companies new to the area and keen to be part of the local community.

Others could be voluntary groups whose interests and aims are similar to your areas of strength, or they could be sympathetic to the projects that your school wishes to develop.

There could also be individuals known for their philanthropic support of good causes, or there may be celebrities – sportsmen, musicians, authors – who either live locally or who have been connected with the school in the past.

There are also local organisations – Mayor's Appeal, branches of Lions, Rotary, Round Table, etc. – who will support, and help to raise funds for worthwhile initiatives in their community.

Case study

A special school in Suffolk was working on a small-scale scheme to provide a hydrotherapy pool when their local newspaper, *The Lowestoft Journal*, who annually support a local cause, offered £120,000 funding – but the funds had to be used within a year. This offer of funding was the catalyst to develop a bigger project, which was soon matched by nearly £200,000 from the County Council.

An approach to the Foundation for Sports and Arts stipulated that the new facilities would need to be made available to the disabled throughout the local community, and so a programme of events commenced involving local groups for the disabled.

There has been a series of fund-raising events, from sponsored cycle events to golf tournaments and in the end a total in excess of £1 million was raised. This has provided an extensive range of refurbishment and building projects at the school, resulting in a gymnasium, additional classrooms, specialist teaching areas, a purpose-built nursery, a physiotherapy and medical room, a sensory room and, of course, the hydrotherapy pool.

Source of contacts

Some of these contacts may already exist within the school. This is really the place where you can start to find out 'who knows who' at your school, and how this network of contacts can be advantageous to your fund-raising.

In order to carry out such an audit, you will need to identify the contacts that currently exist within your school such as:

- staff and governor contacts – here there are obvious contacts from the organisations that your governors work for, whether

as local councillors or in commerce. There are also indirect contacts with relatives (partners, brothers, sisters, etc.) of staff – both teaching and support;
- contacts through parents – most secondary schools have on average 1,000 pupils and so there are probably at least that many contacts with local employers or possibly national companies with local branches;
- curriculum contacts – in certain areas within the school, contacts may have been already established with local concerns, such as:

  - school trips to factories or service utilities;
  - work experience – an annual event in most secondary schools where over 200 pupils spend up to two weeks experiencing the working patterns of local companies;
  - regular presenters, from outside agencies, for assemblies, etc.

- local and national suppliers – schools can be important customers of many businesses whether locally (glaziers, paint suppliers, grounds maintenance or hardware stores) or nationally through catering, utilities, classroom supplies or through maintenance contracts. As a valued customer your relationship with these concerns is already established and can be used to mutual advantage.

You may find possible resistance to some of the information being sought. It can be construed as an invasion of privacy. However, much of this information is already supplied by parents' emergency contact details, held by the school's support staff.

Also, there is no need for you to use this information in a personal manner. For example, if it is known that a significant percentage of parents are employees of one local company, then this can be valuable information for a fund-raising project leader.

Sources within the local community

Bear in mind that although your internal sweep may well provide you with a wide range of contacts, experienced fund-raisers always stress that there are as many unexplored contacts on your doorstep. You should never overlook the local environment in which your school operates.

There may be occasions when your initiative needs the support of your LEA, or their involvement may enable you to enlist further support from other local government departments.

Similarly, local, national and European political representatives can be valuable supporters or conduits through which helpful contacts are made.

Open meetings to discuss your fund-raising projects may attract like minds and, as problems shared are problems halved, representatives from local groups who have similar dreams and aims. Such allies may be able to help in staging fund-raising events.

Case study

When a school in Dudley started on their journey to gain over £4 million of Lottery funding for their community Arts and Sports complexes, they began, at an early stage, to network with:

- local and regional arts/sports groups;
- local disability groups;
- council departments for Arts, Sports and Leisure;
- local businesses;
- governing bodies of various sporting agencies;
- officials of specific sports and arts organisations;
- local councillors/officers and MPs.

What are the benefits of closer ties with local organisations?

Everyone who becomes a partner in your fund-raising initiative does so for a good reason. In each instance there will be a different factor which influences prospective partners to join you in your quest. (In Chapter 2, these were referred to as WIIFM factors.)

While these factors are often distinctive, there are overall headings that can be used to see how the main beneficiaries, the community, the schools and commerce, in these schemes will gain.

Benefits for the local community

There can be concrete benefits, such as improved facilities, greater opportunities to put on entertainment or events, or improved educational opportunities for all ages. Other, less tangible, benefits include 'community spirit' and 'neighbourliness', and an improved communication base for the local community.

Using local celebrities as project champions (not solely from sport or the media) can give your initiative a welcome boost. Again, you have to be able to convince these busy people not only of the local benefits that success in this venture will bring, but also of how their involvement can be seen as a positive move on their part.

Benefits for the school

Similarly, schools will benefit from new or refurbished facilities, extra resources, and the release of core funding for 'school-only' purposes. Other benefits include the shared experiences, the opportunity to develop project management skills, together with the experience of 'managing the boundaries' – a concept now encouraged in education management training for school managers, whereby the control of external influences on schools is considered as important as internal issues.

Benefits for commerce

Often the involvement of businesses in fund-raising in schools is seen as having ulterior motives, such as influencing teenager spending or accessing future employees at an early age.

Sometimes there is a case for appeasing a 'social conscience' and there may be instances where some companies have received unfavourable press coverage and can redress the balance by becoming involved in projects supporting schools or charities.

There are also certain tax benefits to be gained especially if the project has a charitable aspect, as well as various training or vocational opportunities for business personnel (e.g. ICT, languages).

Case study

A deputy head at a community college in West Sussex believed that there were strong arguments for local partnerships with commerce including:

- to inform companies of the qualities and abilities that today's school-leavers possess;
- to involve potential college governors from business and industry;
- to embrace recent government initiatives that encourage partnership between schools and commerce;
- to take advantage of businesses that are actively seeking to support educational and community schemes;
- to improve local opinion of the college.

To date, the college has established partnerships with the following:

- HSBC Bank, setting up a College Midbank where students can manage and involve themselves in setting up savings accounts, and sponsoring the college prospectus.
- McDonald's who sponsor an attendance project, and have contributed new rubbish bins. The local restaurant manager is also now a college governor.

The college continues to host termly Business Breakfasts – sponsored of course – attended by local companies, pupils and staff and is currently seeking support and partnership for the following initiatives:

- a National Lottery bid for just under £1 million to enhance community sports facilities on the college campus;
- gaining Investors in People status;
- an IT project with the Worshipful Company of Information

Technologists (yes, it really does exist) and Syntegra for local small and medium-sized enterprises (SMEs).

So there are benefits for commerce and the community, from initiatives developed by a college whose motto is 'Achievement through Partnership'.

Maintaining your contacts database

You need to be able to ensure that you can guarantee confidentiality to parents, governors, staff and other bodies providing you with contact details, and maintain such details in accordance with statutory requirements.

Similarly, you must have the technology and skill to maintain and utilise a computer database, using current software that ensures you can search, sort and match data as easily and quickly as possible. You certainly do not want to waste valuable time trawling through a manually updated card system. Both the database and its accessibility need to be an asset to your fund-raising initiative.

Developing contacts with existing agencies

One of the best agencies to start with is your local Education–Business Partnerships (EBP). These partnerships are supported by the DfEE, and local County Councils, and have close ties with local Chambers of Commerce, Enterprise Agencies and Training and Enterprise Councils (TECs).

EBPs will not only welcome you, but will also act as a valuable source of contacts, having been involved in many initiatives which encourage links between education organisations and local businesses, such as:

- industry days;
- work experience;
- practice interviews;
- business visits;
- teacher placements.

Details of your local EBP can be obtained from a national organisation called Business in the Community (BITC),[1] the UK's leading authority on Corporate Community Involvement. The mission statement of BITC is: '[to] inspire business to increase the quality and extent of their contribution to social and economic regeneration by making corporate social responsibility an essential part of business excellence'. It has recently published *The 1999 Examples of Excellence* in which there are details of various programmes which 'demonstrate the measurable impact a company can have on society both through its community programmes and its business' (Sir Peter Davis, Chairman, Business in the Community).

One of the programmes cited by BITC as an example of excellence is Face 2 Face with Finance, a leading edge programme developed by NatWest.

Case study

NatWest realised that its success depends on the ability of individuals and organisations to manage their financial affairs effectively. This has been endorsed by research which found that:

- a majority of teachers and parents thought that money management should be taught at school, and that banks should play a role;
- young people wanted to learn about managing money at school.

In consultation with teachers, NatWest has developed a programme of ten modules for secondary schools and colleges to teach money management and enterprise skills. Fully trained NatWest staff work with teachers to help plan and deliver the programme. Support materials are professionally printed and provided free of charge.

Since the programme was launched in 1994, over 130,000 young people have benefited. Independent research from

> NFER shows that the programme is having a positive impact on young people's financial literacy skills.
>
> The impact of the Face 2 Face programme can be expressed thus:
>
> - 50 per cent of secondary schools have been actively involved in almost 8,000 activities;
> - Face 2 Face has increased students' understanding of relevant concepts and helped develop students' key skills in planning, problem-solving and communication;
> - staff involved with Face 2 Face show significant improvement on their competencies, raised morale and improved work-related skills.
>
> (BITC, *The 1999 Examples of Excellence*)

BITC has acted as facilitators, encouraging corporate social responsibility in many other examples where support from business concerns, both locally and nationally, has made a difference.

Contact with your local EBP can provide more detail relating to these examples and other local schemes where partnerships between industry and education have benefited schools and the community.

Local community centres, clubs and societies

There are many organisations in your locality that can either offer direct support such as Arts Centres for arts projects, or Community Centres for social awareness schemes. Some may have been in existence longer than your school such as museums, churches or local history societies, and while they may only be able to provide indirect assistance, some of their advice can provide a direction which can prove very fruitful.

Case study

When a primary school in South London was looking for ways to celebrate their centenary year, they became involved with a local photographer's gallery. Between them they came up with a project which would combine research into the personal history of the pupils at the school with state-of-the-art technology, especially in respect to photography and ICT.

The project gained the support of a local charity, the Walcott Foundation, who supported initiatives which combined educational issues with new technology, and also sponsorship from Kodak. This interest gained further support from two more charities, Sir John Cass's Foundation and the Gulbenkian Foundation.

The project has received support in the form of equipment, expertise and funding in excess of £20,000, and has enabled the school to become pioneers in Internet usage in primary education, where the pupils have been able to display their work on their own website.

Note

1   See Appendix 1 for contact details of BITC.

Chapter 4

How to match up with funding agencies

By now you should have prepared the ground for fund-raising in your school in a thorough, open and creative manner, but nearly all your work so far has been concentrated on local issues. As your fund-raising quest continues, now is the time to identify the many staging posts, detours and avenues that exist for schools to explore. These are opportunities to become involved with initiatives, programmes and organisations that have been established to further educational themes and develop partnerships.

The opportunities detailed in this chapter are neither exhaustive nor comprehensive. It would be impossible to cover every eventuality in detail. The purpose here is to provide sufficient information for you to know where to go next, whom to contact and the style of approach to take.

There are now many more chances to gain extra funding than were available a few years ago. This is partly due to the concept of partnership funding, especially in the public service sector, and partly due to the change in approach from schools where entrepreneurism can now function more freely.

Funding agencies available to schools

Probably there are a lot more of these than you thought. Some are for major capital development projects, others for curriculum development initiatives, while some schemes are carefully focused on a particular social, environmental or commercial theme.

This chapter is divided into four sections:

- government funding initiatives;
- European funding initiatives;
- grant-awarding trusts;
- commercial support in education.

Government funding initiatives

The Specialist Schools Programme

The Specialist Schools Programme, originally launched by the DfEE in the early 1990s, was re-launched in July 1997 with new criteria to reinforce the role of schools as a focus in the community. The mission of this programme is to develop schools as centres of excellence for the teaching and learning of specialist subjects.

The programme is open to maintained secondary schools only, whether they are LEA-funded, foundation or voluntary-aided. There are currently four areas that these schools can focus on:

- Technology;
- Languages;
- Arts;
- Sports.

The programme enables schools, in partnership with private sector sponsors, and supported by additional DfEE funding, to build on a particular strength, developing a distinctive identity in their chosen specialism. The aims of the programme are:

- to extend choice and diversity in secondary schools;
- to offer new choices to parents and students;
- to strengthen links between schools and business;
- to help raise standards of teaching and learning in the specialist areas.

Every school applying for the programme must do the following:

- draw up a development plan;

- commit itself to measurable performance indicators and quantifiable performance targets;
- raise sponsorship of around £100,000;
- build ongoing links with sponsors.

The DfEE makes two grants available in this programme:

1 an initial capital grant of £100,000 – matching the raised sponsorship;
2 additional funding of £100, for each pupil studying the specialist curriculum area, per year for an initial period of three years. This amount is capped at £100,000 per annum.

   From September 1999, specialist schools will receive an extra £20 per pupil per annum, capped at £20,000, to support further work with other schools and in the community.

This programme uses the school's development plan as a starting point, and encourages all schools who have a strength in a parular curriculum area to develop this with the assistance of the LEA and commercial partners.

For Sports and Arts Colleges, funding from this programme may also qualify as partnership funding for a school's bid for National Lottery funding.

Case study

A secondary school in Kettering was halfway through a £1.2 million Arts Lottery bid, when the Specialist Schools Programme was extended to cover Sports and Arts Colleges. This resulted in an opportunity presenting itself to the school to combine aspects of the Lottery submission with a bid for Arts College status, centred on performing arts and media.

In 1997 the school was successful in both bids and a building programme has commenced for a £1.7 million Community Arts Centre, incorporating a £100,000 media centre funded by a DfEE capital grant.

> The proportion raised by the school is in excess of £400,000, made up of 50 per cent from LEA grants, 25 per cent from commercial funding and discounts, 17 per cent from trusts and foundations and 8 per cent from local fund-raising events.

As at December 1998, 330 specialist schools have been created, of which 227 are Technology, 58 Language, 26 Sports, and 19 Arts Colleges. This number is expected to expand to around 500 by September 2001. Specialist schools have enjoyed the support of over 100 LEAs, located in rural, urban and inner city areas.

Affiliated to this programme are the TC (Technology Colleges) Trust[1] and the Youth Sport Trust,[2] whose purpose is to act as co-ordinating and advisory bodies. They have separate divisions for advising on curriculum development plans and for sponsorship. Publications issued by these Trusts include lists of all schools that have benefited from this programme. These provide vital points of contact and networking.

Since the TC Trust was launched, over 300 companies, foundations and individuals have contributed over £60 million to schools in this programme, including over £25 million between 1996 and 1998.

A word of warning, however. The location of your school is one important factor to be taken into account. Applications which are not close to existing specialist schools, and those from areas of social deprivation, may be given preference.

If you already have a specialist school in your area then you will need to show how your application is different and will bring diverse benefits to the local community.

Schools can now access all the information on the Specialist School Programme on the Internet through the DfEE website at www.dfee.gov.uk/specschl.

Public Private Partnership (PPP) projects in schools[3]

This programme is administered by the Schools Private Finance Team, at the DfEE in London. They work closely with the Public Private Partnerships Programme (4Ps), a company set up by the

Local Government Association (LGA) to advise schools and LEAs on the potential of Private Finance Initiative (PFI) schemes.

The PFI was launched in November 1992 in order to foster new relationships between the public and private sectors, especially in relation to new building projects. The two key strands to this policy are:

- to introduce private sector efficiency and management skills into the ownership and maintenance of public sector assets;
- to encourage the private sector to provide capital for the construction or maintenance of buildings or facilities in the public sector.

Throughout the 1990s, this style of funding for capital projects has met with more success in the National Health Service and Department of Transport than in Education. This has a great deal to do with the difference between the size of population served by NHS Trusts or road/rail users and those catered for by individual schools.

The management style encouraged in schools over the past decade has been one of independence, particularly with the advent of grant-maintained/foundation status and the concept of local management of schools initiated in 1988.

Hospitals, however, have been encouraged to become large trusts, serving sizeable populations, and road/rail PFI schemes have been established to meet the needs of large sections of the UK population.

The intention behind this programme is that the cost of either new buildings or building refurbishment will be covered by a consortium, usually made up of several commercial concerns who undertake to deliver and maintain the required facilities for the LEA who will then lease them back from the consortium over a set period of time.

The benefits to LEAs are that facilities are provided which can be funded over a period of time instead of demanding an immediate capital outlay. To the consortium the benefits relate to high predictability of the 'income stream', in this instance funding from those authorities whose responsibility it is to provide state education.

Case study

In February 1997 Dorset County Council became the first LEA to sign up for a PFI scheme. A consortium of nine private companies won the contract to build and maintain a brand new comprehensive secondary school in Bridport. It will also run certain services such as catering, grounds maintenance and cleaning, over a period of thirty years.

The new school will replace the very first comprehensive school in Dorset, built over forty years ago to accommodate 650 students. Numbers are expected to rise to over 1000 by the millennium and the project will provide state-of-the-art facilities and buildings at a cost of around £11.5 million.

Negotiations for this project have been ongoing for a considerable time and, as with any pathfinder project, many lessons have been learnt on the way. Managers with the LEA and the school are now sharing these experiences with other schools by hosting seminars on the experience of PFI deals.

Funding for projects

DfEE funding for these projects is either in the form of:

1 'PFI Credits' which provide revenue support to LEAs to help meet private sector charges;
2 capital grants through the New Deal for Schools (NDS) Programme;
3 for voluntary-aided schools only, also in the form of annual revenue grant to meet private sector annual charges.

For some projects DfEE may provide support for external professional fees.

Progress to date

By mid-1999, there have been ten signed Public Private Partnership deals for schools in the following LEAs: Dorset,

Kingston-upon-Hull, Hillingdon, Dudley, Enfield, Kent, Lewisham, Leeds, Portsmouth, and Waltham Forest.

PFI schemes are part of the DfEE's £5.4 billion capital programme from 1999 to 2002. There are a further twenty-nine schemes approved by this programme's Project Review Group plus a further thirteen projects that have been approved by the DfEE for NDS funding but have yet to be signed.

Contact details are given in Appendix 1.There are a number of publications available on this programme, a list of which can be obtained from the School Private Finance Team. Initially, full details, and copy of some of these publications, can be obtained on the Internet (www.dfee.gov.uk).

Both *Support for Schools: A Guide for Employers* and *Public Private Partnerships – A Guide for School Governors* are available from DfEE Publications.

The New Deal for Schools (NDS) programme

This special five-year programme was launched in July 1997 by the DfEE following the Chancellor's Budget statement making £1.083 billion available to education. Some £680 million has already been allocated to improve the condition of school buildings – £83 million in 1997–98, £257 million for projects that began in 1998–99 and £340 million for projects beginning in 1999–2000.

The remaining £400 million will be allocated to projects commencing in the remaining period up to 31 March 2002 when NDS funding will cease.

This funding is intended to cover the following areas:

- the backlog of repairs in schools;
- improvement to security in schools;
- facilities for technology.

This funding can also be used in conjunction with projects involving Public Private Partnership schemes designed to ensure that schools are repaired and maintained in the long term.

It is currently recognised that there is in the region of £3–4 billion worth of work required to be done on all state schools throughout the UK in order to bring them up to a satisfactory standard, so while this level of funding does not match the recognised need, a fair amount of this work can be addressed by this programme.

Although it is early days, indications suggest that this funding will go to the most pressing building issues. Some of these come under the banner of health and safety, or just overdue refurbishment, such as ensuring that no pupil has to go outside to visit a toilet.

Every year, LEA Chief Education Officers are being encouraged to establish Asset Management Plans (AMPs) which will highlight where school building needs should be addressed in their area.

These plans will also prioritise the schemes put forward by schools. LEAs will therefore need input from schools on their individual plans in order to submit the most pressing cases to the DfEE for funding.

Bids should do the following:

- demonstrate how educational standards will be raised;
- provide for renewal, repair or improvement of school buildings;
- ensure that access, inclusion and sustainability are fundamental factors;
- benefit from matched funding (15 per cent);
- cover only schools in either the voluntary or LEA sectors;
- demonstrate good value for money.

Your school needs to be able to develop such building schemes, closely following the criteria under which funding is available.

Details of the Condition Categories and Suitability Assessment can be found in Annex A and B of the notes covering Phase 4 of the NDS programme, again available on the Internet at www.dfee.gov.uk/newdeal.

More importantly, schools need to work closely with their area LEA personnel and be fully prepared, at specific times of the year, to be able to submit well-prepared and thought-through plans which can not only match the specifications of this programme but will also be able to attract the requisite matched funding.

The National Lottery

The good news is that this is undoubtedly one of the most exciting funding opportunities for education in the 1990s. The bad news is that it takes a lot of hard work to make a National Lottery bid work, and then a great deal of time and effort to deliver the scheme. But, then, doesn't everything in life that is worth striving for?

However, many of the schools who have had Lottery bids approved have found the secondary effects of such schemes to be as valuable. These benefits include increased community involvement, improved staff morale, better commercial links, and raising pupil achievement – and you get money too.

If you don't believe that National Lottery funding is for your school, then look at the list in Appendix 3, of the top 100 schools who have been awarded Lottery funding. The list shows levels of awards from £290,000 to just over £4 million, and there are hundreds of schools who have gained awards under £300,000.

In this guide, details relating to the National Lottery are concise. The purpose of making such funding available is to 'make a difference to the quality of life for all people'. The greater the participation from the local community in your project, the greater the chance of funds being awarded. All National Lottery projects must be of a high quality, represent good value for money, and the end product must have a duration of many years.

Each Lottery application will need to show that the project meets a need that overcomes a shortfall in existing facilities, especially with regard to the needs of the local community.

There are currently six grant-awarding bodies within the National Lottery organisation, the original five:

1 the Arts Councils;
2 the Sports Councils;
3 the Millennium Commission;
4 the National Heritage Memorial Fund;
5 the National Charities Lottery Board.

The sixth body, the New Opportunities Fund, was created in 1998.

The Arts and Sports Councils

These Councils have been the main recipients of Lottery bids from schools, often in conjunction with sports clubs, Arts Centres and connected local groups.

Most bids involve a portion of matched funding and schools would be prudent to assume that they will be required to raise in the region of 20 to 35 per cent of the project value. For projects under £100,000 this can be reduced to 10 per cent, but this is at the discretion of the Arts or Sports Councils.

In general, for every Arts bid there are currently seven Sports bids, and Sports bids can take over six months to process, with Arts bids taking rather longer.

The procedures for submitting bids are very specific and non-conformance to these rules will result in failure. However, bids can be re-submitted and several schools, having failed at the first application, have learnt from this, and gained awards on re-submission.

In both areas, Sports and Arts, developments on funding opportunities are dynamic and change from year to year. In January 1999, the Arts Council of England launched a new Stabilisation Programme, committing more than £50 million over the next three years to this initiative.

Similarly, the Regional Arts Lottery Programme, administered by the ten Regional Arts Boards, awards grants of between £5,000 and £30,000 for the following areas of work:

- education;
- access, particularly for the less able;
- production and distribution;
- investment in artists.

Again, the two best approaches for information, forms and advice are either to contact your Regional Arts Board or Sports Council, or surf: www.artscouncil.org.uk; www.english.sports.org.uk; or www.lottery.culture.gov.uk.

Arts For Everyone (A4E)

From 1996 to 1998, the Arts Council ran a fast-track option for Lottery funding, A4E, mainly aimed at smaller groups starting up new projects rather than capital ventures. Although this programme has finished, it is useful to refer to it as it proved a valuable learning exercise for many schools, charities and other non-profit-making organisations.

It may be prudent for schools to dip their toes in the fundraising pool by taking on a small-scale project, maybe working with a local arts/community group to develop an initiative in creative and performing arts which couples the school's strengths in this area with meeting a local need. This could be in the form of artist workshops, a drama competition or a series of dance performances from local and national companies.

Case study

A school in Bexley gained a £5,000 award from A4E to develop a 'combined arts project exploring the identity of the local community through the eyes of the pupils, their parents and grandparents'.

The project, for younger pupils, used photography as a medium through which students could produce images of their community, presenting their work utilising all the multimedia facilities available at the school.

Support, both financial and in kind, was given by local and national photographic concerns, and the award has enabled the school to offer an enriched curriculum while also meeting two of the A4E criteria – encouraging participation in arts activity, and getting more young people actively involved in arts and cultural activities.

National Heritage Memorial Fund or the National Lottery Charities Board

There are few opportunities for schools to make bids through these organisations. If the school building has, for example, listed status or the school is closely connected to a charitable organisation who will benefit from funds being made available, then it may be worth investigating possible funding schemes from these bodies.

The Millennium Commission

This Commission has allocated all the funds at its disposal, and there are no future opportunities for schools to obtain funding from this source.

The New Opportunities Fund (NOF)

This is the sixth National Lottery grant-awarding body, established by the government in the latter part of 1997. Funding is available for initiatives involving Health, Education and the Environment. NOF works in partnership with other organisations to support sustainable schemes that can do the following:

- improve the quality of life for individuals and communities;
- promote social inclusion;
- encourage community involvement;
- complement and enhance relevant, regional and local strategies and programmes.

The first three initiatives to become available for funding (applications up to Spring 1999) were as follows:

- information and communication technology (ICT) training in education;
- out-of-school hours education and childcare activities;
- a core network of healthy living centres.

In October 1999, the first set of awards, for out-of-school hours study support projects, were announced with more than £2 million being shared between ten schemes covering over 100 schools. These schemes included:

- a new cyber café in Kirklees;
- additional sports and arts activities in Tower Hamlets;
- expansion of a homework and computer club in Sunderland.

Details of successful bids can be found on the NOF website at www.nof.org.uk, together with guidance notes for both study support funding and DfEE Standards Fund money, where LEAs can apply for a range of grants available to undertake school improvement through targets agreed with LEAs through Education Development Plans. Details of such grants are available on the DfEE website.

By the end of 1999, NOF will have launched three new initiatives:

- cancer treatment and care;
- community access to lifelong learning;
- green space and sustainable communities.

Awards for All

As a follow-up to A4E, a straightforward 'one phone number, one form' way to bid for National Lottery funding has been set up for charities and arts, sports and heritage groups. It is called Awards for All and community groups can apply for grants of between £500 and £5,000 without worrying about which of the distributing bodies to go to. From April 1999 the number to contact in England is 0845 600 2040 and in Scotland 0645 700 777.

General advice and contacts

Most successful schools have shown perseverance and determination to gain their awards, and many of them are willing to pass on their experience. You can search the Lottery website for awards by area, amount date of award or type of award. Then it is up to you to make contact with some of these successful organisations to see if they are prepared to share the secrets of their success.

There are also bodies, such as the Directory of Social Change,[4] who can offer advice and contacts for such assistance.

European funding initiatives

The opportunities to gain funding through European sources are somewhat limited and some of the sources that existed in the late 1980s and early 1990s no longer do so. For example, RESHAR, RETEX and KONVER were EC programmes designed to overcome the economic and social consequences of the downturn in particular industries – coal-mining, textiles and the defence industries in each instance – and all these programmes were scheduled to finish in 1997. Direct contact with the European Commission[5] (UK offices) or the Department of Trade and Industry[6] will clarify the situation.

Certain schools were able in the past five years to take advantage of funds available from such schemes. The Garibaldi School is one of the best examples.

At present, if you believe that your school is in an area where changes in employment may make EC funds available, then do some research through your Chamber of Commerce, Business Links and the DTI to set up your case and to see what may be available – not forgetting the contacts and awareness of EC programmes from your local MP and MEP. The EC stipulates that all member states should be responsible for funding nursery, primary and secondary education.

Possible EC funding opportunities involve developing co-operation and initiatives at a European level. Therefore schools will need to find partners for projects from fellow member countries.

Funding from the EC has to be matched at around the 50/50 level. Initiatives in specific curriculum subject schemes, such as language exchanges or in technology, are strongly encouraged. The Socrates[7] series of funding programmes has been available to schools for some years, and promotes the following themes:

- school partnerships and co-operation in general;
- improved knowledge and use of EU languages;
- co-operation between EU institutions at all levels.

Making contact with organisations which will guide you through these schemes is recommended, and subscription to bodies such as Eurodesk[8] can be an excellent way of keeping up to date with EU opportunities.

Case study

In 1996, a high school in Durham embarked on a joint project with a co-educational secondary school in Morteau, France, to investigate similar problems encountered in both countries relating to water shortages.

The project involved trips, with their French counterparts, to the Centre for Alternative Technology in Wales and recruited assistance from both universities at Durham and Sunderland.

The standard of research and the content of the project, especially regarding the experiences offered to the pupils, both in schools liaison and the school trips, resulted in the school winning a prize of £5,000 from the Franco-British Council.[9]

Teachers from Languages and Technology departments in both schools took part, together with twenty-eight pupils. The project is still in operation, and the school has also enjoyed a trip to the House of Commons to receive their prize.

The teacher in charge of the project commented that winning the money had not just enabled the pupils to acquire new experiences, but had also strengthened the school's knowledge of project management, as well as extending contacts with other education establishments both in the UK and abroad.

Grant-awarding trusts

Trusts which can offer funding opportunities to schools are usually found under the following categories:

- general purpose trusts who have among their aims the support of educational projects;
- trusts established by commercial enterprises which often have a specific social or environmental focus;
- minor trusts that exist, sometimes locally, which have funds set aside for educational purposes only.

General purpose trusts

Some of these organisations have become household names in recent years. The annual BBC Children in Need Appeal,[10] Charity Projects (Comic Relief)[11] who organise the Red Nose Days, and the Prince's Trust[12] are all such grant-making bodies.

Often schools do not believe that they can apply for funds from such bodies, but this depends on the type of project or the focus of your fund-raising strategy. Yet a school can stand a much better chance of attracting funding if they are working with voluntary sector agencies.

If, for example, your project involves pertinent youth issues such as drugs, employment or truancy, then there may be scope to attract certain like-minded grant-awarding organisations.

The ADAPT Trust,[13] for example, is strongly involved in ensuring access for the disabled, particularly to Arts premises and, as this is often a strong focus of Arts Lottery guidelines, there may be certain common ground which could interest this Trust.

Likewise, there are many of these Trusts, often set up by philanthropists some decades ago, such as Wolfson, Gulbenkian and Nuffield, whom you may be able to interest in your specific scheme. Similarly, celebrities are now establishing Trusts which can offer funding, such as the Sir Cliff Richard Trust and the Cameron MacIntosh Trust. These Trusts are very specific regarding the type of support they are willing to provide.

Often your scheme or project will need to have an activity focus rather than that of providing a facility, and in the above instances the activity would need to be connected to music/musical production.

Commercial trusts

Such Trusts have come more and more to the fore in the past decade as major corporations develop a corporate conscience. Sometimes organisations in a particular industry combine to form a grant-awarding body. For example, the companies involved in the football pools business established the Foundation for Sports and Arts, which has assisted many local groups in supplying equipment or facilities.

Other individual companies have decided to focus on specific areas. For example, the Paul Hamlyn Foundation concentrates its support on the Arts, education and book publishing and welcomes project details for schemes involving after school arts activities or literacy projects.

Minor or local trusts and foundations

This can be a bit of a treasure hunt. There are instances where bequests and legacies have been made by local residents for educational purposes. These often apply only to schools within either the parish or borough in which these people lived, and often have specific covenants as to their use.

The funds that they offer may not be substantial, but they can have an important role in assisting with feasibility planning or 'pump-priming' a project to interest other grant-making organisations.

Publications such as *The Directory of Grant Making Trusts* or *A Guide to Local Trusts*, should be available in most libraries or through Business Links, usually allied to local Chambers of Commerce. Other sources could be through local historical societies, churches and museums.

Commercial support in education

Having already noted that commerce is beginning to take a much more active role in supporting schools, there are six different ways in which this support has arisen in recent years:

- direct sponsorship;
- competitions;
- provision of resources or materials;
- developing community schemes;
- supporting curricular or education issues;
- through Education–Business Partnerships.

Direct sponsorship

Companies have become school sponsors particularly in the Specialist Schools Programme. Among the 300 or more concerns who have pledged over £25 million to this programme, there are national concerns such as Rolls Royce, British Airways, Dixons, British Aerospace and the HSBC Financial Services Group, together with a wide range of local companies.

Similarly, examples can be cited where commercial partners

have provided matched funding in National Lottery bids for community facilities based in schools.

Many major concerns now issue documentation which covers their approach to education. For example, BT have a document entitled *Working with Education*, detailing their provision for curriculum material, their Teacher Fellowship scheme, the BT school link scheme and other BT education initiatives.

Competitions

Throughout the year there are competitions for schools organised by companies, sometimes with cash prizes, or for specific curriculum resources. Details of such competitions can be found in the regular educational publications such as *The Times Educational Supplement*, *Schools Funding Update* or in the education sections of daily newspapers such as the *Guardian* or the *Independent*.

Prizes range from £100 to £10,000 but often, as someone once said, it is the taking part that is more important than winning. The experience gained in these competitions can range from becoming a focus of interest, to pride and commitment and, on occasions, fun!

There are competitions for essay writing, public speaking, poetry, school newspapers, technological inventions, environmental concern, and social causes, not to mention 'Teacher of the Year' nominations. These competitions can spark a great deal of interest from local companies or local branches of national concerns.

Provision of resources or materials

There are two ways in which companies run programmes which provide resources for schools:

1 By collecting tokens when the public purchase goods from them. The best known of these schemes are those run by food superstores such as Tesco and Sainsbury's to provide computers to schools. Other companies run similar schemes but here tokens can be exchanged for books sports equipment or musical instruments.

2 By the direct supply of materials. This is not a common occurrence but the ICI/Dulux Community Projects[14] scheme gave £180,000 worth of free paint away in 1997 to voluntary groups and charities in the UK.

Developing community schemes

In keeping with the growing 'community conscience' that certainly major corporations are beginning to exhibit, there are good examples of opportunities where a school can develop community or environmental programmes with funding from commerce. For example, the Barclays New Futures Initiative[15] provides cash and resources for school/community partnerships. Some eighty awards were made in 1998 to secondary schools, worth either £3,000 or £7,000 in cash, for programmes developed by the school which met the set criteria.

Barclays Bank have worked with the CSV[16] (Community Service Volunteers) since 1995 on this initiative and have made over 240 awards in that time.

By supporting curricular or education issues

Commercial enterprises may choose to favour a particular curriculum subject. For example, Lloyds/TSB have set up the Artsbound[17] initiative which is designed to offer opportunities to pupils to experience the Arts at first hand.

Here, Lloyds/TSB will assist in the cost of school trips to the National Gallery or local galleries, and have expanded their scheme now to include classical music concerts and theatre performances.

Similarly, Allied Domecq sponsors courses in schools throughout the UK entitled 'Understanding Industry' and has funded a national programme, through the CBI, for training for careers education and guidance.

Through Education–Business Partnerships

Education Business Partnerships (EBPs) have been set up throughout the UK to provide a single framework through which education and business can develop and enhance links.

There is a great deal in the way of advice, contacts and useful links available at your local EBP. They are ideally placed to be marvellous facilitators in your funding strategy (see p. 40).

They have close contacts with Chambers of Commerce, Enterprise Agencies, TECs or LECs, and the Business-Link departments of the DTI. If they cannot help you directly, then they probably will know who can.

General comments regarding commercial support

There are several general points worth considering before approaching commercial enterprises, whether local or national, as prospective project partners.

Develop the business contacts that already exist

In most secondary schools, there are programmes, such as the Trident work experience schemes and Young Engineers Associations, through which links with local industry and commerce have already been established.

These are precious contacts and they should be carefully nurtured, especially with details of contact names, areas of expertise and support. Details of all these contacts should be kept on your database for use in developing partnerships.

In a future scheme some of these contacts may not be able to become sponsors, but they may be able to contact other possible sponsors with details of the values and strengths of your scheme. Or they may be able to assist with support in kind, such as expertise or equipment loans.

If, as a primary school, these contacts are not available, liaison with your local secondary schools could prove positive and lead to joint resource ventures.

Similarly, details of suppliers to the school, whether local or national, should be recorded in this database. These contacts – who require business from your school – can be useful sponsors even at a low level of funding – maybe to sponsor a fund-raising event, or a brochure for your project.

As in the work experience scenario, sponsorship has to be mutually beneficial, and with local companies, good PR for good causes can be a welcome change to the standard methods of sales promotion.

Target organisations that are interested in you, and your project

It is true that many companies now include educational support in their corporate statements, but there are often occasions where this support is heavily qualified, so it is recommended that you research their statements before you contact them. Kellogg's mainly offer support for educational initiatives in the Manchester and Wrexham areas – areas close to their factories.

Thus, if you have a project for an Arts complex based on a school campus with landscaping opportunities, then it may well be worth approaching concerns with a track record in supporting the Arts and/or education and/or environmental issues.

However, for the building or refurbishment of Science laboratories, perhaps either the petrochemical industry or the energy companies would be a more productive route.

Look for opportunities which will be in the interest of the prospective sponsor

Sometimes there is a great deal of serendipity and coincidence connected with finding the right sponsor at the right time. (See Case study on pp. 17–18.)

It is not always down to chance, however, and often schools can make their own luck by targeting sponsors with common interests, using local community and school contacts, and by doing their homework.

Schools need to know whom to approach; who makes the decisions; what are the core functions of companies; and how are they doing. Some companies may be expanding in your area. Some may have experienced bad publicity recently. Some may have a poor environmental record. All these may be opportunities for your school to redress the balance in their favour. Much of this information may be available from your local newspaper.

Operate from a successful position

Most of the success stories have taken place in schools who identified their curriculum strengths through their development planning and then matched their resource initiatives to these plans.

Your school may be a regular prize winner at Drama or Music Festivals or Technology Fairs, or some of your pupils may go on to play sport for professional teams or represent their country.

You may have staff with ambitions in areas of Science or Art who can use these opportunities to realise special commissioned works incorporated into resource schemes.

Any of these strengths and assets are launch pads for your fund-raising initiatives and will impress and interest prospective partners. Everybody likes to be associated with success.

Be inventive and use lateral thinking

Projects need to have an appeal, just as business ideas have to have something that sets them apart from the competition. There needs to be a 'special ingredient' that interests prospective partners.

This may be the support of a local personality or national celebrity; a connection with a local charity or just an idea which no-one else has thought of before. It would be even better if a group of pupils had come up with the idea! Sometimes there are connections in your local area, just waiting to be made.

Finally, use creative acquisition. The fairly comprehensive list of schools included in the Technology Colleges Trust brochure will probably disclose schools nearby that have established successful business partnerships.

Scan the local press for articles on successful initiatives from schools involving business support. Seek them out and ask their advice regarding approaches, contacts and the lessons they have learnt.

Be professional, positive and patient

Developing long-lasting relationships always needs professionalism and patience, and you have to keep working at it. However, current evidence now shows that the willingness of businesses to participate is very strong and the returns to all partners involved – staff, parents, pupils, sponsors and the local community – can be substantial in educational resource development.

> ### Case study
>
> In 1997 a school in the South of England raised, as part of their Technology College bid, pledges of financial support at around £118,000 from local commercial interests. Maybe this was no surprise in a conurbation with organisations representing the armed forces, shipbuilding, cross-Channel ferries and light engineering, together with a multitude of service industries. The surprise was the money was raised in just three days.
>
> When it was remarked how easy it was to get this level of support, the response from the Head left little doubt as to how much hard work and effort had been involved gaining this support, and how the seeds of this success had been planted some time ago.

How to find out about business sponsorship

Back in the early 1990s, the DES issued a leaflet entitled *Support for Schools: A Guide for Employers*[18] which, besides giving advice on how businesses could give support to schools, also gave reasons why these links should be encouraged. This leaflet, still available, emphasised the importance of local commercial support, the positive statement being made by such support from the local community, and the benefits enjoyed by such partnerships.

In 1993 a publication entitled *Building Effective School–Business Links* was published from work carried out by Andrew Millar from the Centre for Education and Industry at the University of Warwick. This document is still available from Westex Publications free of charge.

More recently, sources of advice and guidance in this field have been published by the following bodies.

The Technology Colleges Trust/DfEE

Secondary schools should have received copies of brochures entitled, *Specialist Schools: Education Partnerships for the 21st Century*. Copies of this publication are available from the DfEE together with the TC Trust brochure.[19]

Any school interested in developing programmes which require partnership funding involving commerce should contact this Trust, even if only for an overview and confirmation that business sponsorship in education is alive and well and going from strength to strength.

The National Consumer Council

This organisation published *Sponsorship in Schools: Good Practice Guidelines* in 1996, covering sponsorship in schools, particularly for materials and activities in schools. This document provides a checklist for teachers, managers, governors and parents, so that the high standards of quality, balance and integrity, expected of educational resources, can be maintained.

Business in the Community

As detailed in Chapter 3, this is a DfEE organisation who publish *Partnership Points: The Education Business Partnership Newsletter* which is full of articles on sponsors and activities which can stimulate ideas for your own school

Business Sponsorship Associations

Finally, there are many organisations which have been established to encourage and develop sponsorship in a particular field. For example, the Association for Business Sponsorship of the Arts (ABSA), is a charity with links with the Department of National Heritage.

ABSA has developed the Pairing Scheme whereby businesses are encouraged to sponsor the Arts. This organisation is worth seeking out for all schools interested in gaining Arts College status through the Specialist School Initiative or National Lottery projects with National or Regional Arts Boards.

Notes

1 For contact details of the Technology Colleges Trust, see Appendix 1.
2 For contact details of the Youth Sports Trust, see Appendix 1.
3 For contact details of the Public Private Partnership, see Appendix 1.
4 For contact details of the Directory of Social Change, see Appendix 1.
5 For contact details of the European Commission, see Appendix 1.
6 For contact details of the Department of Trade and Industry, see Appendix 1.
7 For details of Socrates, see Appendix 1.
8 For details of Eurodesk, see Appendix 1.
9 For details of the Franco-British Council, see Appendix 1.
10 For details of Children in Need Appeal, see Appendix 1.
11 For details of the Charity Projects, see Appendix 1.
12 For details of the Prince's Trust, see Appendix 1.
13 For details of the ADAPT Trust, see Appendix 1.
14 For details of the ICI/Dulux Community Project, see Appendix 1.
15 For details of the Barclays New Futures Initiative, see Appendix 1.
16 For details of the Community Service Volunteers, see Appendix 1.
17 For details of Artsbound, see Appendix 1.
18 See Appendix 2 for publication details.
19 This publication is available from the Specialist Schools Department of the DfEE. See Appendix 1 for contact details.

Chapter 5

Home-base support in fund-raising

In any journey, it is very important to receive solid support from your own organisation. In mountaineering, climbers establish a base camp to which they report back and where they can look for encouragement and support when necessary. Thus, with fund-raising in education it is important that support is exhibited by your school and from your LEA, although this is not always possible as LEA officers cannot and should not show favouritism.

Having enlightened you as to the many and diverse sources of funding for your school, there are two questions which now arise:

- will your school have to provide some funding of its own?;
- in times of financial stringency, where will this contribution come from?

In answering these questions, your school must be willing to show its active support for the chosen fund-raising strategy.

Providing funding of your own

The answer to the first question is yes – there is normally a requirement for schools to make a certain contribution to most initiatives. In most current funding projects, there is often an element of *matched funding* that the school has to come up with in order to gain grants or awards. Certainly, the recent trend in most funding initiatives has been towards the incorporation of *partnership funding*.

This contribution, while sometimes being minor in value, can deliver some major benefits:

1   Commercial and trust partners will be encouraged if the school is seen to be 'doing its bit' in the whole funding equation.
2   The events that are put on to raise these funds, such as shows, sponsored rides, swims or walks, or car boot sales, can have a marked effect on local awareness of your project. They can also help with community relations and importantly be a lot of fun.

Fund-raising events are hard work, but schools often have groups within them, usually made up of parents, teachers and pupils, who can take on this burden. Some of these groups can also have charitable status which can lead to additional benefits such as tax savings or awards from other charities.

Where does the school's contribution come from?

Where can your school find such funds when lack of funding was the main issue that started you down this road? Sometimes there may be a contribution from your LEA, but often they are as strapped for cash as you are. Obviously, this difficulty can be relative to the size of project that your school is undertaking. For example, in the Art for Everyone (A4E) programme, for applications up to £100,000 the matched funding element is at least 10 per cent, whereas a. major Lottery project in excess of £1 million can require matched funding in the region of 25 per cent to 35 per cent.

Likewise, a grant from a Trust may require 25 per cent matched funding, but if the project is for specific facilities under, say, £50,000, then a school target of between £10,000 and £12,500 can be more realistic.

To get started, you may be considering a feasibility project, where the matched element is fairly low and attainable. It may be prudent to start at this level and test the local waters for support and encouragement. If you cannot raise, say, 25 per cent of the feasibility costs, then it is not going to be easy to fund the whole project.

However, be careful that your school doesn't become obsessed with this contribution – many schools are. This is often the first stumbling block in your strategy, so in order to help you respond to the doubters, here are a few pointers.

Does all matched funding have to be cash?

No, in fact in the A4E programme only 5 per cent need be in financial contributions whereas the other 5 per cent can be gifts in kind. And how are 'gifts in kind' defined? The answer depends on who is giving the grant. There are instances when the free-of-charge supply of materials to your project can count, or the discounted value on the supply of goods, or the value of the land on which your facility will be built – you need to check with the body awarding the grant.

When approaching the Arts Council for feasibility funding, the value of time spent by the school in planning and researching a project can be counted towards matched funding.

There have been examples of companies offering free project management expertise to schools, the actual market value of which can also be considered as matched funding.

All in all, there are opportunities for 'non-cash' matched funding in many of the initiatives available to schools, and the advice in each instance is

- read the small print;
- ask whether you can include your 'gifts' as matched funding;
- play by the grant-awarding body's rules.

What if your school has absolutely no money for matched funding?

You don't need reminding that you still have to address the scarcity of funds for your well-documented resource improvement initiatives. This is where the role of the local supporter comes into its own. This role can take many forms.

Local benefactors, whether individuals or organisations, can donate matched funding. Remember, matched funding does not have to come direct from your school's budget – it only has to be found or raised *by the school*.

Local firms, maybe even your own school suppliers, can be a vital cog in the fund-raising process by sponsoring a brochure, or a cheese and wine function, or a beer and skittles evening. During these events potential sponsors and partners can be introduced to the aims of your thrilling and exciting project.

Local companies, making a contribution of a few hundred pounds, say, can become catalysts in your fund-raising project, hopefully interesting other parties that may be able to offer greater support. Remember that a full page advert in a trade journal can cost between £400 and £800, so if you can offer your local supplier a better advertising deal then you can both reap the benefits. Remember the WIIFM factor!

There may be local trusts, able to utilise their funds only for educational purposes in your geographical area, who can assist in a similar way with small 'acorns' of funding.

And finally, there are ways to raise funds throughout the year within your school. Here are details of some of the tried and tested schemes to support fund-raising projects which again can be great fun involving pupils, teachers and parents:

Sponsored events

These can include walks, cycling, readings, knit-ins, swimming, hymn-singing, etc. – really anything that catches the imagination of the local community and in which you can involve pupils, parents, staff, governors, local groups and celebrities. This is the area in which the fun really can be had, and the commitment of the school can be shown to its fullest effect.

Yes, it involves a fair bit of work and organisation, but the prime motive for these events is raising money and the secondary aspects of public awareness, press coverage and community involvement can be even more valuable.

Setting up a trading organisation within the school

Many schools already trade in some way or other, whether it be a tuck shop or the sale of school uniform. The school can set up a separate company to run the total fund-raising project or to make the most of merchandising opportunities (T-shirts, mugs, pens, etc.).

Case study

A school in Derby has established its own trading company which has resulted in extra funding of around £20,000 becoming available each year. The company is centred round a general store, situated in the school, which sells everything from confectionery to stationery, and uniforms to calculators. The trading company has also become involved in catering and publishing contracts.

The turnover is around £120,000 per annum, realising a profit of around £20,000. The school has also established a charitable trust through which these profits are paid in order to minimise the corporation tax liability.

The company employs its own non-teaching staff, together with part-time consultants to cover the legal and statutory issues. The aims of the trading company are to meet the needs of the students on site.

The headteacher, who also acts as unpaid MD for the trading company, states that the school has learnt a great deal about which wholesalers to go to and which to avoid.

The school plans to run a conference for managers from other schools on the advantages of, and tips on setting up, a trading company.

The best advice on how to set up a trading company can be gleaned through local accountants and solicitors – usually recommended by your local Business Link office or Chamber of Commerce – who may already be Governors or appear on your contacts database.

Some of the organisations – referred to later in this chapter under the heading 'networking' – are very experienced in this field having guided many charities and voluntary groups down this path.

There are also promotional companies who can develop advertising revenue, through maps, handbooks, and calendars. Similarly, manufacturers and retailers, for products ranging from uniforms to books, are now actively targeting schools for a substantial part of their business. In many of these instances you can incorporate these promotions, or the trading proceeds, into your fund-raising projects.

Related performances/productions/outings

This can involve special events such as concerts, one-off performances, competitions, galas, etc., where the profits go to the specific project fund. This again is an opportunity to have wide involvement from parents, pupils, etc. and may provide an occasion for ex-pupils to make their contribution, especially if they have become megastars.

The other aspect is gaining sponsorship for extra-curricular events – school plays, concerts, trips and outings – which would normally come from standard school funds.

Securing sponsorship for these events or curriculum related visits is a creative method of finding alternative funding. Here your contacts database may come into its own as a source of potential sponsors.

Covenants

Covenants are legal methods by which parents, ex-pupils, or 'Friends' of the school can make donations in a tax-beneficial way. For example, a parent promises to pay the school a fixed sum every year for four years, the minimum period for a covenant. Often schools approach parents in the year admission for a period of five years to cover the time attended by the student.

Payments can be annual, quarterly or monthly and are usually set up as a standing order. The amount is the choice of the parent and the benefit to school is not only the actual donation but the income tax that has been paid on donations made under the deed of covenant.

Allied to this is the aspect of setting up a charitable trust through which the covenant scheme is administered.

Charitable status

The benefits of having an organisation within the school that has charitable status are two-fold:

- grant-awarding trusts like to give to other charitable organisations;
- a charitable trust within the school can be a convenient vehicle for tax benefits from trading companies or covenant schemes or gifts made under the Charity Aid scheme.

To set up a charitable trust you need to draw up a Trust Deed and register the Trust with the Charities Commission.[1] As such, you will be able to quote a unique charity number.

It may be wise to take up professional advice when setting up such schemes but again there is plenty available, often through education or charitable organisations – see later section titled 'networking'. You may also be surprised how many solicitors you have in your contacts database!

In general, you can consider all or any of these methods of fund-raising either for your contribution to the matched funding element of your project, or as alternative sources of funds to bolster the standard funding available to your school.

In both instances, it is your approach that will win the day – and the funding. And in order to develop your approach thoroughly, you need time and commitment from your project leader or fund-raising strategist.

Making a success of local fund-raising

There are plenty of sources of assistance and advice, mainly because education is well placed to learn from the fund-raising experiences of charities, many of which have become fairly expert in this field over the past decade.

The downside to this is that the whole area of obtaining grants or awards has become vastly more competitive, and in order to overcome this you, like any other organisation, must ensure that your appeal stands out from the crowd.

Creativity

The charities who have been most successful in fund-raising are often those who have been more innovative and creative in the projects that they have developed. Can you imagine Red Nose

Day being such a success if it was run on the lines of a party political broadcast?

Consider a university town where in the past five years many charity shops have been opened within the bustling student environment. All these shops are doing a brisk trade, and the charities in question have spotted a niche in the student market which their shops can fill.

Networking

Major national organisations, set up to support charities, such as the Charities Aid Foundation[2] and the Directory of Social Change,[3] can provide invaluable advice and information. They are beginning to offer first-hand experience and networking to schools, through seminars and journals. Many of their publications are listed in Appendix 2 and should be available through your local library.

Remember too that there are organisations, such as the your local Citizens' Advice Bureau, or Chamber of Commerce or the National Council for Voluntary Organisations,[4] where advice and help can be sought. In all these instances they may not have the exact answers to your needs but they will probably know who does.

Notes

1   For details of the Charities Commission, see Appendix 1.
2   For details of the Charities Aid Foundation, see Appendix 1.
3   For details of the Directory of Social Change, see Appendix 1.
4   For details of the National Council for Voluntary Organisations, see Appendix 1.

Chapter 6

Gaining support for your fund-raising

How to do the asking

This is the difficult bit, but it can be made easier if:

- you are well prepared;
- your focus is clear;
- you are positive and professional.

You need to possess all these qualities because the people you are now going to approach – with the hope of them becoming partners in your fund-raising strategy – will also have all these characteristics. And on top of this you need a bounteous dose of good luck!

This advice is, of course, good common sense. An entrepreneur would not entertain visiting his bank manager or investment brokers without first devising his 'mission statement' and taking along with him copies of his business plan.

While the situation is slightly different – your school will not be seeking a loan – asking for support, whether financial or otherwise, without any obvious dividend to the sponsor, could seem somewhat foolhardy and a little unlikely.

But, however unlikely it may seem, it is happening, and certain schools are seeking out the sort of organisations that wish to be seen to be actively supporting education, and then matching this support with grants from trusts and government departments.

Making sure you are ready for the approach

Is the fund-raising strategy formulated, communicated and realisable?

Does everyone in your school know about your fund-raising initiative? Are you being altogether realistic or maybe somewhat over-ambitious? Have you done all the homework that you need to do at this juncture?

Teachers have both the skill and experience in advising students on how to best approach examinations, interviews etc. Approaching potential fund-raising partners is no different, and the same level of preparation, application and research is required.

Are the aims of your project clear, worthy, attractive and achievable?

Clarity is essential when approaching businesses, and becoming even more so with organisations involved in the National Lottery. If you have identified a local need that the facilities envisaged in your scheme will meet, then make this a prominent feature of your prospectus, brochure or presentation.

The word *worthy* is seldom used nowadays, but it has its place in this context. Your scheme must be attractive, your goals realistic, but even more so your project must be deserving.

Are your prospective partners the right ones for your goals?

The phrase 'horses for courses' may not be appropriate for schools but it is certainly wise to approach organisations whom you know already may have some empathy with the chosen focus of your fund-raising appeal. For example, the Royal Insurance Group is known to be a major Arts sponsor; Panasonic/Technics are major supporters of music-based initiatives in schools whereas Cable & Wireless Plc have supported Technology competitions and initiatives in the past.

However, you may not have either local links with such organisations or there may not be any obvious candidates to support your scheme. This is the place for lateral thinking.

Case study

A new school in Portsmouth, strongly connected with a well-known admiral in naval history, considered different foci for an Arts Lottery bid. One of these ideas was to establish a community radio station on its campus, especially as within the forthcoming year, a new FM radio licence for the local area would be open to bids from interested parties. One of these parties, already known to the school, operated on the local cable network with the station identity being that of the admiral's flagship.

The school was also very close to several industrial estates, with many companies who were involved in maritime products or services. There were also long-established contacts with Marconi Engineering who had one of their main manufacturing sites close by.

The idea of a community radio station on a school campus was novel in itself and with such lateral local connections, as one of the radio people put it, is a marvellous opportunity for excellent synergy!

Have you identified possible problems and made alternative plans?

There are bound to be problems. Recognising this at the start means that there are fewer surprises to come your way. It may be that you have difficulty getting agreement from your LEA, or planning permission may be doubtful. There may be a limited area for development or lack of parking space which could jeopardise the community involvement.

Sometimes it can be very worthwhile to have a 'What if …' session to explore alternatives should things not pan out the way you hoped.

Accountants believe that prudence is a virtue, and in this case prudence or foresight can be seen by the organisations you approach, not as a sign of weakness but rather as an indication that your approach is proficient and thorough.

Kissing the right frogs

So, you are at ease with the preparation you have made, and you are ready to appeal to organisations that could become partners in your fund-raising initiative. As Sir Bob Salisbury, Head of Garibaldi School in Mansfield, comments, 'This is where you need to be sure that you are kissing the right frogs.'

How can you be sure these frogs are the right frogs?

You cannot be absolutely sure, but you can increase the probability of finding yourself approaching kindred spirits. The factors involved are preparation, experience and knowledge.

You have already prepared your case, part of which is scanning all the possible partners whether from commerce, grant-making organisations or statutory bodies.

Information from parents, governors and pupils – work experience can be a vital two-way exercise – can guide you as to which of these could be interested in supporting your scheme.

Maintaining the right connections

There are a number of opportunities throughout the year to welcome your favoured network of contacts into the school. The more obvious events are carol concerts, school plays, open evenings, music competitions, sports days, science days or any other events where the public are invited to attend.

Similarly, there is nothing to stop you inviting your prospective partners in to see the school in action, and you may be pleasantly surprised at the reaction of many businesses who are keen to become part of the world of education.

The main aim here is to keep your contacts informed so that they feel they are a valued friend to the school. Certainly, in work experience initiatives many organisations value the experience of school contact as much as the pupils gain awareness.

Remember that these organisations will have their own reasons for good relations with schools. Pupils are future employees, parents can be possible customers or there may be mutual advantage for a community organisation to be connected with the quality offered in your school.

How are you going to get 'frogs' to turn into 'princes'?

The chances of pure philanthropy are remote, but luck can play a vital role. Schools have succeeded where there is a factor common to the aims of the prospective partner or the school.

As has already been seen – see Case study on pp. 17–18 – schools who excel at languages can attract local or national concerns who may be in the process of a major export drive and need the facilities to train their personnel in particular European languages.

Similarly, concerns with a strong research tradition may be interested in supporting technology or scientific interest especially if they can see that the standard of approach in the school is both proficient and developmental.

Case study

A community college in East Sussex obtained a DTI grant by establishing a partnership with a local ICT provider and a training/PR company based close to the college. The grant of £148,000 was awarded for an initiative called the Micro'borough project and enabled the college to establish four LEARN centres for ICT training, application and practice for students of all ages.

Two of the factors responsible for awarding the grant were that the project would be available to benefit SMEs in the town, and that it would provide a model that could be replicated by other schools.

The incentive for the project came from the college's 1996 Ofsted report which, like many, criticised the college's ICT provision. The college's principal decided not to play ICT catch up but to develop centres that would ensure that the college was a pace-setter in local community ICT training and development.

In both 1997 and 1998 the college has actively taken part in Net@days – a series of events designed to make schools across Europe more aware how to use the Internet and how information and resources can be shared.

The college has also become one of the first in Britain to gain Sports College status under the DfEE Specialist School Programme, gaining support and sponsorship from a consortium of organisations including twenty sports clubs, sports suppliers, the PTA and certain trusts.

How to handle rejection

The only thing you know for certain is that you will receive more rejection letters than offers of help, but as the chairman of a major multinational Japanese concern once said, 'Success is always 99 per cent failure'. There are lessons to be gained from adversity, but before you become comfortable with the sackcloth and ashes, remember that some success is vital to progress your fund-raising strategy.

Very, very few schemes at present do not include a partnership element and increasingly schemes are encouraging this style of project evolution. Working on these partnerships can be as rewarding as gaining funding.

Often the most disappointing rejections can be from those concerns that you may have identified as just the right partners in your scheme. In these cases check your approach. Could there be any chance of misinformation or misinterpretation? Have you done everything you can to try to get them on board or was your approach half-hearted?

In the next section, we look at the recommended way to make an approach, whether written or personal. At present, major companies or grant-awarding organisations are receiving an ever-increasing number of requests for help or funding. Many of these requests can be poorly conceived or use the 'scatter-gun' approach and you need to be careful that you are not tarred with the same brush.

Be careful that your approach is about establishing a relationship – not just asking for funding. You want to explore whether the common ground, that you believe links your school with your selected organisations, is really there.

Many people quote the adage 'It's not what you know, it's who you know' and to reverse this, if you haven't made the effort for organisations to get to know your school, then you will struggle.

How to save 'frogs' for future projects

There are occasions when you get offers of interest, but your specific project is not in line with the aims of the company whom you have approached. You may get a reply which is encouraging, like the following: 'Thank you for sending details of your fascinating and exciting music project. In our corporate development plan we have identified community and education projects with environmental themes as our chosen area of support.'

In this instance, file for future reference for when you are building your small animal enclosure or your wilderness habitat or your inner-city wild-life scheme, but make sure that on every possible occasion this concern knows of your successes, adventures and even failures, put across as learning experiences.

Case study

In 1996, a secondary school in Melton Mowbray began a campaign to create an Eco-Centre at the school. This facility would provide students with first hand experience in alternative energy sources, waste management and water purification.

The management group, set up to facilitate this project, included representatives from partner schools, the local borough council and environmental groups.

The school registered as an environmental body, meeting the criteria laid down by Entrust – the regulator of environmental bodies under the Landfill Tax Regulations.

Environmental bodies are eligible to be funded through a tax credit scheme linked to the Landfill Tax – duty which is paid by landfill operators. These bodies must be non-profit-making private sector organisations, who can then obtain funds which would normally go to the Inland Revenue but which goes instead to a worthwhile school/community project.

The school already had a well-established environmental strategy in place, and so they were able to set up the initiative fairly easily. They had already identified their sponsors, shown them round the school, got to know them and found them to be helpful in dealing with the documentation.

Their professionalism and vision, together with being well prepared and a touch of serendipity in discovering the Landfill Tax scheme by chance, have resulted in the school being able to build the Eco-Centre – thanks to funding support of £37,000 from their sponsors.

Getting the paperwork right

The bodies that give out grants and awards are seeing an ever-increasing mailbag every week from charities, schools, hospitals, youth clubs, local groups and community organisations. Some have reacted by becoming more bureaucratic, others by specialising in the field in which they allocate grants.

There have also been instances where, if you have not addressed your brochure or letter to the correctly designated or named person, it has been filed in the bin unopened.

With this increase in postal traffic coming their way, you need to have some sympathy for these organisations who are often run for charitable purposes by a few dedicated volunteers. You also need to adapt to their requirements.

Completing documentation for grant-awarding bodies

There are five main guidelines to consider when approaching such bodies for funding.

Play by their rules

If your school decides to ignore the instructions when completing what often seem bureaucratic and in-depth documentation, then do so at your peril. It is very likely that the forms will be returned from the grant-awarding agency.

If additional information is requested, or asked for in a specific format, then there is a good reason for this. It may not seem apparent, but experience has already shown that by not complying with instructions you can miss out on opportunities of grants from these agencies.

Read the small print

There may seem to be a large number of grant-awarding bodies who are committed to supporting, say, the Arts or Education or Community Projects, but some of these may be quite specific in the particular area of support that will be granted.

For example, many trusts do not wish to become involved in building projects but may support visits to art galleries, etc. Similarly, some trusts may be limited geographically in that they may only support organisations in a particular district.

In each instance, thoroughly and painstakingly research the charitable objectives and grant-awarding policies of these bodies.

Identify your match

Some trusts may also favour areas of urban regeneration, often in tandem with government and EC schemes, so it is very necessary to know exactly where each trust or foundation stands – you may be wasting valuable time.

Charities like to give to charities

There is often a specific requirement from these agencies that funding will only be granted to organisations who have charitable status (see pp. 70 and 74–5).

It is sensible to ensure that this avenue is available to your school, and the status of your PTA/PSA should be checked, so that it is one of the approaches made by your school when seeking funding.

Take the time to plan your approach

A professional approach, with a well-thought out project, will have a good chance of success, but knowing whom to contact; their position in the agency; and making personal contact, usually by telephone, will put your school in a strong position.

While agencies exist to make grants available, there is still only a finite amount of funding, and more and more organisations are becoming aware of the methodology and approach which lead to success.

As with other areas of education where competition has become a factor when chasing scarce resources, obtaining funding is no different and needs a strong, professional and committed approach.

Advice for dealing with certain partners

Often when you are dealing with Government initiatives, National Lottery bids, or EC funding schemes you will encounter similar hurdles to overcome – seemingly over-bureaucratic forms to fill in and a process that seems never ending.

Although you may feel like giving up before you have even started, take a look at the list of schools who have received National Lottery funding in Appendix 3. In order to be successful in gaining funds, each of those schools has had to do the following:

- meet the relevant criteria;
- fill in all the forms;
- follow through each stage of the process.

If they could do it, why can't you?

Case study

Second in the list of schools in Appendix 3 is the Dormston School in Dudley who in fact have been awarded two National Lottery grants – one for £1 million for a Sports Centre, and £2.94 million for an Arts and Craft Centre.

The impetus for this whole project came in 1993 when the Ofsted inspection report commented on the lack of PE facilities at the school. This coincided with a petition, delivered to Dudley Metropolitan Borough Council, from concerned members of the local community highlighting the lack of leisure services in the area.

The working party, set up to deal with these two issues, consisted of representatives from the school and local borough officers. This group devised a scheme to provide sports and arts facilities at the school, with funding to be applied for from the National Lottery, the Foundation for Sports and Arts, and from European initiatives.

There were many hurdles to overcome, and after two years' preparation and research, a bid of around £3 million was made for National Lottery funding. This was when the work really started. Lottery Officers visited the school, examined resources in the local community and held discussions with borough officials. A further survey covering a wider catchment area was requested, together with an improved business plan.

Later in 1995, sums were pledged from the Borough Council and the Foundation for Sports and Arts – as matched funding – and everything looked cut and dried, until the Arts Council decided that the design of the building was not up to standard.

Here the project gained the help of the Royal Institute of British Architects, who requested leading architects to submit new designs, one of which was chosen in mid-1996. Not only did this new design meet with the Arts Council blessing, but it also included better facilities for both the school and the community – but at an increased project total of £5.5 million. The two awards were made in August 1996, for over 70 per cent of the project total and building work has finally commenced.

The headteacher admits that it has been a tough learning experience, with many false dawns but, with persistence and the support of all the agencies involved, the project has been a great success.

The pros and cons of writing letters

This can be a most frustrating exercise in fund-raising. You have developed a brochure of startling invention and clarity of purpose, using the best printing facilities to give your project the most professional approach you could imagine.

You have attempted to get partners interested. The list of prospective partners has been carefully culled and selected. And then it is obvious, from the replies that you receive, that they have not understood, or perhaps even read, your brochure!

It will happen. If at first you don't succeed do not give up – you will get some positive feedback especially if you follow these suggestions:

1   Do NOT ask directly for money. (It may still arrive, so who's complaining?)
2   Give your prospective partners opportunities to get to know your school – enclose tickets for a function or ask them to come and have a look round the school.
3   Ask whether you can come to see them to talk through your initiative, or suggest that you will contact them by telephone in a few weeks.
4   Enclose a stamped-addressed envelope or an easy-to-complete reply card for their responses. Make it easy for them. Whether it is a charity or a business, everyone is very busy.

Letter writing, sending brochures or mail-shots are important, and are a good starting point. If you have done your homework on whom to approach, then you have made 'first contact', especially if you may be going where your school has not gone before.

One of the bonuses of this approach is that you have informed a sufficient number of organisations, all of which you have identified as suitable as in the past they have supported causes similar to your fund-raising initiative.

Whether they support your scheme or project is down to your persistence, professionalism and possibly creating your own luck. (Review the case studies on pp.17–18 and 79.) But you have informed many organisations, not only about your initiative, but also about your school, its values, its standards, its achievements and its aims.

The pros and cons of a direct person-to-person approach

This can be the most fruitful area but again is very difficult to pursue. Most successful schools have had a person leading their fund-raising initiatives who has excellent communication skills.

Similarly, this person needs to have the vision to see a bigger picture than just at the school, i.e. to match community needs with educational resource schemes and to identify hopeful funding partners.

To be able to make the most of the direct person-to-person approach you must first of all have someone who is at ease with this sort of role – the initiative's salesperson. There is an element of cold-calling involved in such schemes. How else do you get to talk directly to the person who makes the decisions in the company that you have selected as a strong possibility to be a partner? Really, only by finding out – again a matter of doing your research, using your contacts database and simply enquiring.

Similarly, there is a need to understand a salesperson's guile in getting to the decision-maker and then a further need to understand his or her motive in becoming a supporter of education schemes.

There are some schools who are now seeing the fruits of such liaisons; they have actively supported school staff with the resources, especially time, in order to make these connections. (See 'The role of the internal consultant' in Chapter 7.)

The importance of networking

The need to continue to develop connections in your community, and maybe with national concerns or government departments, is paramount in this field, even when there seems to be little response.

In the same way that companies are looking out for new customers, your school has the opportunity to come across new partners everyday. These may be:

- parents of new intake, new governors, companies who relocate to your area or just some of the local community that has never had a connection with your school before;

- other schools who are learning from experience, especially in the area of fund-raising. Most schools have access to regular forums for the exchange of ideas in education.
- organisations such as Arts and Sports Councils, technology/IT groups, community centres and European societies – all of which are part of your local network, not forgetting some of the long-standing establishments such as churches, lodges and local charities.

In every instance, there will be an opportunity to put across the aims of your school and the initiatives that you are undertaking to raise standards and improve the quality of learning.

The BT advertising slogan 'It's good to talk' certainly has a place in the field of fund-raising – never more so than when a fortunate connection appears out of the blue. This slogan may soon be overtaken by 'It's good to surf' as the Internet becomes more and more user-friendly and available. Take on the new technology as part of your project management process. Why not create a website for your fund-raising project?

Advice from good practitioners

Effective fund-raising schemes have now been in place throughout the 1990s. This has meant that valuable lessons have been learnt by many parties involved in these schemes, leading to a wealth of advice that is now available to schools in order to avoid the pitfalls.

There are occasions when these experienced practitioners leave their education duties to front seminars and workshops on fund-raising in education. Whenever the opportunity arises to meet, listen to or network with these people, it should not be missed.

Chapter 7

Assembling a potent fund-raising team

While a great deal of your success will depend on preparation, focus and approach, the choice of personnel involved in delivering your fund-raising strategy can also be key. To this end, you need to have a team which can not only achieve the tasks required to meet your goals but these team members also need to have the qualities to be effective, positive and creative in their specific team roles.

The term 'team roles' is used because it is important that the members do not duplicate each other's work, nor overlook areas which can be crucial to your success. Each team member needs to be aware of what is required from everyone else and it may be prudent to designate responsibilities to each member in the following manner:

Plant	solves difficult problems;
Resource Investigator	explores opportunities/develops contacts;
Co-ordinator	clarifies goals, promotes decision-making;
Shaper	challenges, finds ways round problems;
Monitor/Evaluator	sees all options; judges accurately;
Team Worker	listens, builds, avoids friction;
Implementer	turns ideas into practical action;
Completer	searches out errors and omissions; delivers project on time;
Specialist	provides specialist knowledge or technical skills.

(Belbin, *Theory of Team Roles*)[1]

This theory does not set down that every group has to be made up of a team of exactly nine members, each of which takes on the characteristics of one of these roles. Belbin's work concluded that if all these roles were covered within the team, then the chances of achieving success were greatly enhanced. Many people may be able to take on more than one of these characteristics, but very few would be able to cope with more than two of these roles.

You may recall that in both films, *The Magnificent Seven* and *The League of Gentlemen*, each team member was chosen for their individual capabilities and expertise. In order not to encourage criminal activities, maybe the comparison should end there.

Similarly, it is often thought that a mix of differing characters will produce an effective and creative team and, while the mix is important, team members must be committed, often passionate, about the goals of the project.

They must also be prepared to accept the discipline and formality that exist in project management procedures and routines, especially if you are going to be dealing with organisations who are bureaucratic by nature.

Who should be in the team and who should not?

It is often difficult to recommend an ideal number for your fund-raising team but often a working party with more than eight members becomes a committee. It is the *quality* of membership in your team that is more important than just numbers.

Although a problem shared is a problem halved, there should never be an issue over any team member calling on other personnel – as specialists/experts or as helpers – to assist both them, and the project. For example, there is at present a great deal of experience in dealing with Lottery applications in the world of architects and quantity surveyors, and it is not unknown for such professional concerns to offer their services free of charge at the outset, although they will be keen to include their fees in the final bid or project total. However, the balance of the team, from within the school and from the local community or from the world of education, is extremely important:

From within the school

Often, the best candidates from the school are either volunteers or those who have expressed an interest in developing certain skills in the project management/fund-raising experience. If the project has a curriculum focus, then someone from that curriculum area should be represented.

If there is someone on your staff who is looking for a project as part of, maybe, a training course that they are on or as an additional element of their career development at the school, then they may be worth considering for the team. There is plenty to learn on the project management front together with the bonus of enhancing leadership and communication skills.

To a degree, the higher up the school, the less time is available for school managers to attend meetings, etc. The members of your team must have the time to concentrate on getting the job done. Ensure that the chosen school staff are not already overburdened by extra duties.

Other school team representatives could be governors especially teacher–governors or parent–governors, or support staff.

From outside the school

Members from outside the school should reflect the project's aims, and be of use, rather than be there simply to make up the numbers. Their 'local knowledge' and contacts can be invaluable, as well as offering an ability to see 'the wood for the trees' – sometimes a problem in schools, especially at those educational pressure points of examinations, inspections or open days.

Wherever possible avoid the 'resident committee person' – those who sit on committees but contribute very little – as project management demands a working group with strategic prowess as its creed. The bottom line for your team members must be commitment to the cause.

Local representatives from community groups can be an added bonus, especially if they have had project management experience and have a common interest in the focus of your fund-raising. For example, an Arts Centre Co-ordinator can provide an abundance of knowledge relating to Arts Councils, grant-awarding bodies and other organisations who could help your project

Who should lead the project?

It would be rational if the project leader came from within the school. This tends to engender a greater sense of ownership than if an outside agent or fund-raiser is used. However, the project leader must be furnished with the resources to carry out the task, i.e. time, motivation, etc. (review pp. 26–8).

It is tempting to entitle this section of the guide: 'Never let the Head lead the fund-raising project'! In all schools Heads and Chairs of Governing Bodies are very busy, and will rarely have the time to see a project of this substance through in a dedicated manner. But they can have a role to play, often as an inspirational figurehead. One headteacher compared herself to Charlton Heston, playing the lead role in the film *El Cid*. You may remember that in the final battle of the film, El Cid has died, but in order to inspire the troops to victory, he is wheeled out on his trusty steed, with a broom-handle for support. If your Head, hopefully alive and well, appreciates this role, then do not hesitate to wheel them out for visiting VIPs, ensuring they have been fully briefed, perhaps taking care where the broom-handle is fixed!

Setting up a working party

With some school Governing Bodies having between fifteen and twenty members, it is not unusual for schools to have become used to being run by committees. In the case of fund-raising initiatives you cannot afford the luxury of becoming a debating society. In fact, the debates should have already taken place during the planning process. The aim of your fund-raising group is to realise the school's fund-raising strategy by providing the means to achieve the goals.

Making sure you convene a focused working party, where each member knows their expected tasks and responsibilities, is more useful than creating just another committee.

Manage your working party to success

In most schools there are meetings for every conceivable reason, and so you must make sure that meetings of the working party are positive, effective, and well managed. In particular, use positive communication.

Recognising that there will always be doubters is a good start, but always emphasise that the success of this project will very likely lead to further success. This style of fund-raising has been successful elsewhere – why not at your school?

The role of outside agencies, professional fund-raisers or consultants

The use of educational consultants has increased substantially in this decade and very much so since the introduction of Local Management of Schools (LMS). Schools are using their financial independence to utilise the skills of specialists in many areas of school administration.

However, in the list of members of the Society of Educational Consultants you will only come across a handful who refer to resource improvement or fund-raising as their specialism – although more may be involved in industry–school links.

There seems to be two main reasons for the apparent scarcity of resource improvement consultants. First, this is a fairly new concept. While lack of resources may have been around in education for some time, the style of approach, involving partnership funding and promoting initiatives incorporating trust or National Lottery funding, is a recent development.

Second, with funding remaining scarce, schools are loathe to spend valued funds on consultancy fees when classroom resources are urgently required or repairs needed on buildings.

Where extra funding has been made available, it has often been the case that the type of expenditure the funding covers is specific to areas such as teacher training, special needs or curriculum development – all valid and needy areas but not for consultancy fees.

Where to find consultancy help

So, is there a role that such consultants can play and, if so, where can your school find such help? Such consultants can offer a fresh approach, together with the time, focus and expertise in fund-raising to achieve the following:

- develop approaches that will increase the possibility of success;
- develop partnerships between commerce and education;
- liaise between regulatory bodies, i.e. LEAs, Lottery boards;
- develop and encourage links with local community groups;
- complete bid documentation and grant applications;
- offer project management from initiation to hand-over.

If you are looking for advice on choosing a consultant then the recommendation is to acquire a copy of the guidelines issued by the National Council for Voluntary Organisations (NCVO).[2]

Similarly, there is guidance from the Society of Educational Consultants, the Association of Fund-raising Consultants and the Institute of Charity Fund-raising Managers.[3]

Much of this work has come from the experiences of charities, and other voluntary or non-profit-making organisations who have not only honed their fund-raising skills in difficult economic scenarios, but have gained invaluable experience in using consultants.

Many independent schools have appointed appeal co-ordinators who have had many years of fund-raising experience in the charity world, and encountered the quantum shift from fêtes, coffee mornings and raffles (still valid in the new millennium) to the new approaches of corporate support and partnership funding.

However, beside the possible shortage of funding for consultants' fees, the other drawback to using outside agencies could be a lack of understanding of the world of education.

Those who have experienced management in both education and commerce, believe that there is a culture difference which needs to be recognised. Education has differing priorities from commerce, or even charitable organisations, and has not been as focused on the 'bottom line'.

The concept of 'value for money' is relatively new to most schools. However, it certainly is a vital criteria in most new Government initiatives, and National Lottery bids consider this concept to be essential.

The role of the internal consultant

An internal consultant can be a teacher, a governor, a member of the school's management team or a member of the support staff – really anyone who has the time, ability, commitment and energy to see a fund-raising project through to a successful conclusion.

The value of an internal consultant is the ownership of the fund-raising strategy. Outside agencies may well have the expertise and contacts, but will have different priorities and agendas than your school. In most project management training, the emphasis is on the organisation 'owning' the project and this also applies in fund-raising.

In the following example a teacher established contacts with businesses in his local community and developed these contacts to the benefit of both the school and the participating companies.

Case study

In what is believed to be the first instance of its kind, the Governing Body of a state school in Taunton has appointed a full-time fund-raiser. The initial brief for the fund-raiser is to find additional funds for building works which have been completed, but which have been paid for by church funds – a part of which needs to be reimbursed by the school.

This fund-raising in reverse has proved problematic, but the fund-raiser has spent the first year of his appointment carrying out vital marketing and public relations work on behalf of the school.

Contacts have been made with many local and national companies and presentations made to local businesses on what the school has to offer to the local community. As the fund-raiser points out, the future workforce of the area is being educated at the school.

So far, financial support has come in the form of sponsorship for school sports teams, but there has been a remarkable effect on the staff at the school who have found that there is now a conduit for fund-raising ideas, whereas before they had neither the time nor direction to develop such schemes.

There has certainly been a greater interest in the school from the local community since this appointment was made, and much of the foundations have been laid for future success.

This case study may suggest that schools should avoid using external fund-raising experts. Not always so, but the advice is to have the best of both worlds with, maybe, somebody in the school having the responsibility and 'ownership' working closely with an expert fund-raiser.

Leaving it all to either party, internal or external, is not to be recommended but your school needs to be aware of the resources – time, motivation, experience and initial financial support – that will be required to utilise the skills of both.

The role of a project champion

A project champion is someone, well known to the general public, who is willing and able to support your fund-raising campaign. They can be media stars, sporting champions, local or national politicians, or maybe experts in the field connected with your fund-raising focus.

Ex-pupils who have become successful in commerce, politics, sport or the world of entertainment can be a godsend. Their contribution may again be limited to their presence at functions, fêtes or galas which can increase not only interest but also funds.

Case study

In March 1998, a secondary school in Dartford was allocated an Arts Council National Lottery award of over £1.6 million – North Kent's largest ever award – to build a community arts centre at the school.

The centre will provide facilities for performance,

recording and rehearsal, covering a variety of musical styles including ethnic arts programmes.

A symphony orchestra, choral society and amateur operatic and dramatic society will be able to use these facilities, together with the Kent Music School.

The name for this facility – an overwhelming choice by the current students at the school – will be the Mick Jagger Arts Centre. Mick Jagger is, of course, the lead singer of the Rolling Stones but is also the school's most famous ex-pupil. He has also taken a keen interest in the project, following its progress closely.

How to ensure that the team remains positive

So, you have chosen the members of your team or you have sent out invitations to the people who can form a working group to achieve the goals of your fund-raising strategy. Remember that your strategy must have realisable aims and that it can be dealt with in manageable stages. However, the main issue will be good positive communication and the interpersonal skills of the project leader.

Communication

It is vital that dialogue is always available to the whole group. Team members should be given regular feedback, and the opportunity should always be there for them to make their opinions known. This will encourage ownership, and ensure that everyone is up to speed with the scheme.

This doesn't mean that the project has to be riddled with meetings. There are also many more effective communication tools now available such as e-mail or faxes.

Meetings

Meetings should be focused and workmanlike; short and to the point. Yes, there will be areas and issues that require debate, but these discussions can be carried out in a more informal and relaxed environment. Don't let them slow down the business element of your initiative.

Remember that meetings should report on actions that have been carried out, and decide on future actions to be taken.

Roles

It is worth repeating that team members should be aware of their individual roles and also the roles of others. This can ensure that many of the aspects of the project are covered and provide support and respect between team members, remembering that the team performance will also be dependent on the skills and qualities of the team leader.

How to ensure continuity and progress through teamwork

Often there is a great deal of enthusiasm at the beginning of a fund-raising project but once the work begins in earnest, or a few setbacks are encountered, the morale of the team drops and the eagerness begins to wane.

One of the ways is to celebrate reaching each of the milestones identified for the project. Celebrating achievement at each stage of the project can kick-start the next development, and so on.

Remember also that you, and your team, are not alone. You can develop communication tools to inform others about the project, such as:

- Newsletters, which can now be easily put together with current PC software. You may be able to get one of your local suppliers to sponsor the cost of printing, delivery, etc.
- Competitions, maybe for a logo or mascot for the project, or pictures of how the scheme will look on completion. These will keep the project high on the agenda of pupils, parents, staff and the local community.
- Other opportunities to publicise your project, and its successes, from the well-known 'thermometer'-style target to school open evenings and displays in local libraries.

These will not only serve to remind your team of the success achieved, but you will be reaching out to many other possible project supporters, prospective partners who have expressed interest, or pupils and parents at your school.

Many successes have been due to a large dose of serendipity, and there is no reason why your project should be any different.

However, if your initiative is poorly publicised and kept in the confines of your school, then this luck is less likely to come your way. You may not agree with lotteries, but you won't win unless you buy a ticket.

However, when you are setting out your stall, whether at the local library or on your open day, be professional, patient and positive. Much of your success, and your dose of luck, will depend on how you manage your project.

Notes

1 R.M. Belbin (1993) *Team Roles at Work: A Strategy for Human Resource Management*, Oxford: Butterworth-Heinemann. Reprinted by permission of Butterworth Heinemann Publishers, a division of Reed Educational & Professional Publishing Ltd.

2 For details of the National Council for Voluntary Organisations, see Appendix 1.

3 For details of the Society of Educational Consultants, the Association of Fund-raising Consultants and the Institute of Charity Fund-raising Managers, see Appendix 1.

Chapter 8

Managing your fund-raising

Making sure you reach your destination

In your fund-raising quest, you have now explored some of the possible answers to your original questions, such as:

- WHY do you wish to set out on the journey to realise more funding for your school?
- WHAT should be the focus of your project?
- WHERE can you go for advice and expertise?
- WHICH avenues are available to schools for fund-raising ventures?
- WHO will you include in your fund-raising team?

Now the last question to answer is HOW. Some advice has already been proffered – whether relating to your fund-raising approach or where to start.

In the case studies, many of the establishments have not only achieved their fund-raising goals but have also become aware of the secondary benefits from these schemes such as improved educational standards, increase in the number of pupils choosing their schools and a much better relationship with organisations in their local community.

In this chapter, details are given of some of the project management pointers that can assist in moving towards a position of success.

Make sure your project is *SMART*

This acronym stands for Specific, Measurable, Attainable, Relevant and Timely. Your project should be all these.

Specific

Has your project got a clear focus? Are the aims of your fund-raising project easy to describe to a third party? Clarity comes with distinct purpose. Is this the case with your project?

Measurable

Have you put in place the staging posts on which your fund-raising achievements can be measured? This is not only sensible, so that your successes can be celebrated, but also useful in impressing partners of your progress. In showing your ability to meet pre-set targets you will be sending out a message of professionalism, proficiency and conviction.

Attainable

Are the goals of your fund-raising strategy realisable? Do your aims have a chance of success? This may seem somewhat obvious but it is worth considering. Your school may not have experience of such a large project before, and you may be prudent to try out your strategy on a smaller scheme – making your mistakes in an environment that your school can cope with.

Is there anything that would threaten the progress of your project? For example, if you are planning an Arts Centre at your school where parking for the public may be a problem, then maybe think again. Remember hurdles like these are there to be overcome, not to act as a barrier to success.

Relevant

Obviously, the aims of your project will need to meet the needs of your school but are they also relevant to the area in which your school exists? For example, does your strategy dovetail with a recognised need in your local community? As shown in the case study on p. 22, if you want to develop an Arts project at your school, your cause will be strengthened if you are also meeting the needs of local Arts groups.

Timely

Is there a problem with funding which is only available for a specific period of time, maybe within the next twelve months but your scheme will need funding for a much longer period?

Is there a change in local government about to take place which may effect your project? Can you combine your scheme with other projects currently operating in your local community?

Having a mission

The project should have a 'mission statement' which is clear, short and easily understood. Mission statements have had a chequered career in commercial circles. All the rage for corporate concerns one year, and panned by management gurus the next.

Like most management tools they have their good and bad points, but the mission statement may work for your scheme, so don't be afraid to try it.

Case study

When a secondary school in Hampshire was considering an Arts Lottery bid, it began by holding discussions with the Leisure Services at the local city council to find out the Arts needs of the local community. Following these talks, it was decided that the project would be music based and it would have the following mission statement: 'To enable musicians from the local community to have the opportunity to compose and perform, whether as individuals or ensemble, from conception through practice and rehearsal, to recording and performance, on one campus.' This statement had the effect of fine tuning the project so that the design of the facilities were relatively easy to put across to architects and designers.

Similarly, the various parties involved in the project such as the school, the council and local community groups were all singing from the same song-sheet (pun intended).

> Finally, it facilitated the manner in which the project could be communicated to potential funding partners, and also to identify which community partners might be interested in the scheme.

Being able succinctly to lay out the objectives of your initiative, on one side of an A4 sheet, is not only a very positive exercise for your team to be able to clarify your objectives, but it can also act as a useful document to include in proposals to prospective partners or grant-making bodies.

If a mission statement works for your project, it can be a valued component in expounding the purpose of the scheme, detailing the recognised needs and how the facilities will meet these needs.

However, do not make the statement the be-all and end-all. Fund-raising projects are developmental, and as circumstances change, aims may alter and your approach needs to be flexible enough to adapt to these changes.

Having the 'right' targets

It cannot be emphasised too strongly that having targets that meet both the needs of your school and the local community can positively help in most major initiatives.

Certainly, in National Lottery bids, the Specialist Schools Initiative and the New Deal DfEE schemes, the focus is definitely on partnership development for schools. Schools are once again being strongly encouraged to be a focal point within their local communities.

However, this can sometimes be difficult when it is not always apparent who your project partners may be, and a little creative forecasting may be required. However, forward planning is never a bad thing and may often eliminate some of the less desirable outcomes.

Remember also that if there is an existing body which is responsible for the funding of the aims of your project then you are unlikely to be able to access funding elsewhere. For example, the National Lottery is very clear that its funds should not be used *instead of* state funding.

And, finally, do not be concerned if your targets are developmental. The requirements stipulated by certain grant-awarding bodies may require a gradual approach and this style may be in line with the ethos of your school – again playing to your strengths. For example, you may find that by expanding your Arts project to over the £500,000 value, you are then able to apply for feasibility study funding which may help you to develop your project, especially if this is virgin territory for your school.

Establishing milestone and target dates

A wise man, when asked how to eat a whole elephant, replied: 'In small chunks and not all at once!, and your project needs to follow the same logic. To a school whose fund-raising experience may have been limited to school fêtes and PTA events, in themselves excellent forums for raising both funds and awareness, then a National Lottery bid of hundreds of thousands of pounds can be somewhat daunting.

So split your project up into manageable chunks and, to continue the analogy, make sure that each chunk is well digested before you start on the next.

At present, the UK Arts Councils are one of the major grant-awarding organisations that recommend specified stages for the development of projects – from feasibility through planning to implementation.

These steps, together with the simplification of bidding, pioneered by the Arts for Everyone and Awards for All schemes, have encouraged organisations to become better project managers. It can only be hoped that other grant-awarding bodies will follow suit in the near future.

Consultants will offer differing approaches but their ideas are relatively similar. Here is an example of how you could sub-divide your project.

Recommended fund-raising project stages

1   Developing the focus

    (a) for the school;
    (b) for the local community;
    (c) for the relevant associated bodies.

2   Creating a 'mission'

    (a) THE 'mission statement';
    (b) draft plan and specification.

3   Identifying partners

    (a) authorities/statutory bodies;
    (b) potential users;
    (c) project partners;
    (d) project champions.

4   Clarify design specification

    (a) full detailed facilities;
    (b) revenue plan;
    (c) staffing requirements;
    (d) full business plan.

5   Contacting prospective partners

    (a) Trusts/Foundations;
    (b) businesses;
    (c) associated organisations;
    (d) statutory bodies.

6   Courting your partners

    (a) develop your support;
    (b) set targets;
    (c) use your champions.

7   Submit bids

    (a) keep to the bid specification;
    (b) answer all questions clearly;
    (c) supply all documentation requested;
    (d) meet the deadlines.

Source: (ERIC)

As with a great deal of project management procedures, these stages represent common sense and prudence.

However, the emphasis on clarity of focus in the first instance will help your school when identifying prospective funding partners and then the approaches that you should make in order to get them involved.

Show that you can manage your resources

There is a definite need to be able to show clearly how good your budgeting and resource or financial management are, not only for the project itself, but also because it gives your organisation a great deal of credibility.

In many of the application forms, especially from trusts and grant-making organisations, there will be a requirement to report on the financial status of your school. It is therefore prudent to have this done once and once only. Find a format that is readily acceptable in most financial areas (most schools have an accountant on their governing body who should help in this matter) and keep it updated from year to year.

Similarly, certain schemes will require projected income generation and expenditure detail for the facilities that you wish to establish at your school. Here again, your financial acumen, when presented clearly and logically, will hold you in good stead when you have to discuss potential finance with commercial organisations. This is common sense, but it is worth highlighting for three reasons:

1   Education has relied on others to do 'the figures' for many decades and it is only recently, since the introduction of LMS, that the importance of keeping good financial information has been realised.

2   This is no different from the world of commerce where companies are requested to submit their accounts on a regular basis for scrutiny by other organisations, especially those who are making loans or offering credit terms.

3   In each of the project stages, you want to ensure that you only do the work once. It has already been recognised that one of the main problems encountered by schools is the time available to dedicate to your fund-raising strategy.

It therefore makes sense that you should design information, that will go out to LEAs, commerce, parents, etc., in a format that is easy to read, produce, amend and distribute.

It is unlikely that an application for a personal loan or mortgage would be accepted without producing evidence to suggest that the repayments could be met, nor it is likely that companies would get loans if they did not produce business plans in conjunction with their loan applications. The same logic applies here and schools should not think that either someone else will provide this information or that they are exempt from these disciplines.

Monitor the progress of your project

Monitoring does not have to mean checking up, but can be used positively to celebrate success. By using a step-by-step process in your project there are often some stages which must be completed before others, and it is only prudent to ensure that these are completed in order.

There are also often dates for applying to grant-awarding bodies. Some will consider bids throughout the year, like the National Lottery, but often boards of trustees of Trusts and Foundations meet quarterly to consider applications.

Similarly, statutory and government bodies have annual deadlines for funding and certainly the New Deal DfEE schemes run to very specific timetables.

All these factors mean that time management becomes an absolute requirement in managing your project and that is why the role of Completer (see p. 91) is very important in the team.

Yes, deadlines have to be met, because if you submit your bid after the designated date, it will not be considered and then it is all a waste of time, effort and opportunity. Finally, there can be a remarkable sense of achievement that can be gained from meeting the deadlines and completing the project stages.

Ways of overcoming some of the hurdles

Finding funds can never be guaranteed, but you can be certain that there will always be hurdles to overcome – some expected, some not – but there will also be ways to remove, go round or get over them. Often the only difficulty is identifying the right solution for you.

The best advice is to seek advice. Continuing to network will find shared experience which, even if not relevant to your scheme, may generate an idea for the removal of a stumbling block which was preventing progress in your initiative.

Other education establishments (schools, universities, colleges, or LEAs), EDPs, TECs, libraries, the Citizens' Advice Bureau and Community Centres may be willing to help you find the missing piece to your jigsaw.

Within your own school a brainstorming session or ideas forum may bring the solution. Often these are the most simple or obvious, and they may help to keep your project on the right lines or move it in a new direction where success may be more achievable.

There are many organisations such as the Charities Aid Foundation and the Directory of Social Change who have a immense amount of experience in fund-raising, and if there is not an obvious answer they may be able to put you in touch with someone who is involved in a similar project.

Perseverance is the key word in fund-raising projects. There are few examples of success first time round, although there have been some lucky coincidences.

Some of this good fortune has been generated by schools whose approach has been characterised by a clear focus, a known community need, and a strong awareness of the partners that they believe would be interested.

Using a project management consultant

Not only are there plenty of schools who have successfully raised funds through projects involving partnership funding, community association and government initiatives, but there are more and more project management consultants who are recognising that their expertise can be of as much use in public services as in commercial enterprises.

Case study

In a high school in Bolton, the Head, recognising the lack of fund-raising expertise in the school, hired a professional consultant. The first task carried out by the consultant was to do an investigation on the funds the school needed to raise and for what purposes. This resulted in an initial target of £150,000 being set, together with a plan of action which involved the strong support of the school's parents association.

The focus of the fund-raising was a new sports hall, and meetings were set up in which plans were laid out for all interested parties. All the work for these meetings – the displays, documentation, brochures, handouts, etc. – was designed and produced by the consultant.

These meetings raised support from the LEA, the local sports community, and nearby primary schools. This support encouraged the school, especially the parents, to forge ahead with fund-raising events which, with local donations, ensured that the target figure was passed, eventually standing at £160,000. These endeavours have now been matched by a £100,000 grant from the Sports Council bringing the project close to a point of delivery.

The Head is adamant that the project would not have succeeded without the professional input of the fund-raising consultant and, while there were initial reservations regarding the cost of such consultancy, the investment has proved worthwhile.

There has been hard work from the project's supporters group – the staff and parents – and vital support from the LEA but, with patience, and on occasions a thick skin, the project has reached its goal.

Learning from others' experiences

Everyone has become used to the more direct sales techniques in certain commercial fields. One or two of us may have stopped to think how thick-skinned telephone sales personnel need to be after they have interrupted the umpteenth teatime of possible customers. There is certainly no need for projects to be marketed in a similar manner, but there is a great deal to be learnt from positive sales techniques in commerce.

The more innovative companies have focused their sales campaigns on clients whom they believe will be interested in their products, rather than a scatter gun approach. They have identified the benefits that their products can offer, and these are the foci of their campaign.

Your fund-raising aims need to be attractive, desirable and creative. State schools have only recently entered the world of marketing, and while some still have a lot to learn, many are taking these lessons into the area of fund-raising and finding that the success rate can be as high as in the world of commerce.

Chapter 9

Keeping the fund-raising momentum going

This final chapter is concerned with assessing the achievements of your fund-raising, identifying the lessons that your school has learnt from your fund-raising journey, and how these experiences can be used in future schemes.

Have you reached your fund-raising destination?

This is of course very dependent on where you wanted to go. This is an obvious statement, but one which has been emphasised throughout this guide. In Chapter 1, the question of where to start brought out the values of doing your homework at an early stage in order to identify the aims of your fund-raising initiative.

Throughout the early chapters of this guide, it has been continuously stressed how important it is to choose your fund-raising focus, and how this focus needs to be in line with your school's strengths and matched to your local community needs. Being able to have clarity of focus at an early stage will enable you to assess the success of your project.

This clarity assists greatly in identifying which schemes or funding initiatives are open to your school and which organisations may support your cause. In Chapters 6 to 8, the approach that your school takes, and the style of fund-raising that you decide to take, will assist you in reaching your objectives.

There are obvious ways of judging whether the aims and objectives of your fund-raising strategy have been achieved:

- your new building may be built or classrooms refurbished;
- you may have reached your funding target;
- you have received confirmation of a National Lottery grant;
- you may have started your literacy programme;
- you may have enabled a group to visit a theatre, an art gallery or made an exchange visit with another European school.

All of these, and many more examples, will bring your project to a satisfactory conclusion, having raised extra funding to 'make it so'. However, the ends will only be satisfactory if the means have provided both experience and achievement to your school.

Why do you need to keep the fund-raising going?

Fund-raising should not be a one-off experience. The success of your first project is the hook for future partners. Organisations like to be associated with success, and your school's ability to show that it can achieve its targeted resource aims will help to bring more partners on board in the future.

There are also many lessons to be learnt from the experience of your first fund-raising scheme, from community contacts to project management. These should not be filed away as completed assignments, but utilised in many of the other initiatives that your school can be involved in.

Many schools have found their first fund-raising project has been a springboard for other initiatives, not always involving finance.

More and more curriculum areas are welcoming commercial support, which can be linked to grants from Trusts and Foundations. Literacy and numeracy schemes are coming to the fore to match initiatives involving computers and new technology.

Similarly, social issues, already covered in the pastoral education offered in schools, are finding funding support from the 'social conscience' of many businesses, linking with trusts, such as the Prince's Trust and Barclays Bank 'New Futures' Programme, to make a difference in the local community.

The school's local profile is usually heightened in such initiatives, and as you have made more friends and partners, they too will proffer ideas for you to consider as future ventures.

Case study

The community college in East Sussex that gained Sports College status and has become a focal point for local ICT training with its LEARN centres (see case study on p. 81–2) has continued on a fund-raising programme that has netted over £1 million in three years.

Following their initial success the college has gained the following awards:

- an Arts for Everyone award of £5,000 in May 1997 – in a scheme involving artists in residence working with college Arts students;
- in the area of after-school activities, the college has gained awards from Education Extra in the last three consecutive years, together with £1,000 from the Prince's Trust in recognition of their after-school study facilities.
- environmental schemes have also benefited the local community, with the college winning an Eco-School award from East Sussex County Council, and winning a £7,000 grant in the Barclays 'New Futures' programme.
- the college takes part in the DfEE Independent-State School Partnership, working closely with a school in nearby Mayfield, earning the college £19,000 extra funding, while maintaining close ties with the University of Sussex in Brighton.

In most case studies, one common element has been the passion of the fund-raising missionaries. Many comment on how staff in their own schools are beginning to develop their own departmental fund-raising ventures using the same strengths and approaches gained from whole-school initiatives.

Likewise, they are pleased to note that some of the secondary educational benefits can be measured in terms of improving standards, such as:

- an increase in annual admissions to the school;

- a decrease in truancy rates;
- an increase in examination performance;
- a decrease in vandalism and repair costs;
- an increase in pupil opportunities for curriculum or pastoral visits.

Case study

A Berkshire secondary school has turned failure into success. When it failed to secure either a Technology College application or a Millennium Lottery grant, it used the experience to become national pace-setters in ICT provision in schools.

It was during their work for Technology College status that the school attracted support from companies such as ICL, Panasonic and Griffin & George. These partnerships resulted in donations of state-of-the-art ICT equipment, enabling the school to become fully conversant with the educational opportunities of the Internet.

Attending conferences on opportunities for European funding has resulted in obtaining funding under the EEC Lingua project which has financed work experience in Italy, and a link through the Internet with a school in Sweden. This link has resulted in an environmental project which has gained the further support of both local borough and county councils.

The in-house facilities developed by the school, through these initiatives, are able to offer ICT training to the local community.

The school is continuing the strategy, learning from their experience – including their mistakes – and intend to put in again for Technology College status, and to consider applying for a National Lottery bid to improve their sports facilities. Good luck to them.

How can your school keep the strategy going?

As detailed earlier, your fund-raising strategy needs to be part of, and a counterpart to, your annual development planning process. In the same way that subjects such as pupil development, academic achievement and school performance are now monitored year-on-year, so must fund-raising. Your school needs to celebrate its successes in this field – however small – and use the experiences to improve its resources.

Although there has not been any research carried out on the topic of the benefits of fund-raising schemes, there is a consensus that the secondary benefits of such projects – improved staff morale, better community involvement at the school, raising educational standards – are a major incentive for continuing such a strategy.

There may be opportunities during school training days to involve other staff in such schemes or have a debate on the success of your first scheme to see whether there are staff ready to take on the lessons learnt in new ventures.

However you approach it, keeping the strategy alive will enable your school to reap all the benefits of such schemes.

Keeping contacts 'warm'

Projects will always throw up contacts who express an interest in the school but may not have a part to play in your current project. Keeping a database of these for future reference saves a great deal of time and effort in future projects.

Ways to keep these contacts informed and in touch with the school have already been covered (see Chapter 3) but it is important to make sure that all the good work does not finish when your first project achieves its goal.

You could develop a 'Friends' Association at your school with copies of regular newsletters and hold social gatherings. Even better if the newsletter is sponsored by a local company, and written and edited by the pupils at your school.

Some of the DfEE initiatives involve commercial sponsors becoming members of the governing body, and the lesson of getting to know both your local politicians and LEA officers will reap dividends.

In short, your school must continue to network with commercial organisations, grant-awarding bodies and others who can help your school to improve its resource base.

This guide has shown that there are plenty of schools who will not accept the current situation of under-funding in education. It also has provided your school with many examples of the types of funding initiatives that are available to schools.

Keeping up with educational newspapers, magazines and journals may not always be high priority, but in these publications you will not only find more examples of organisations bucking the under-funded trend, but also contacts and details of conferences and seminars where more information and assistance can be found.

It is hoped that the success of other schools will encourage you to set up your own fund-raising strategy, and that, following the recommended approaches and advice proffered in this guide, you will begin to formulate project ideas for your own school.

In conclusion, fund-raising in education can be considered to be more than just a money-raising exercise but it needs commitment from school managers and teachers who may just occasionally have to be bold and take risks.

Sir John Harvey-Jones would say, 'Make it happen', and Captain Jean-Luc Picard on the bridge of the Starship *Enterprise*, would command his crew to 'Make it so', but maybe the best advice comes from Sir Bob Salisbury, headteacher at Garibaldi School, Mansfield: 'Modern schools need teachers who have the courage to shake off the handcuffs, take risks and make mistakes.' Many schools have taken up the gauntlet – why not your school?

Here is a list of general guidelines for fund-raising in education:

- the project needs to have clear, achievable aims;
- projects should have their roots in school development planning, based on sound educational values;
- the project has to be worthy of support, and be attractive;
- the project should be based on an area of success or known expertise within the school;
- in certain circumstances there is an absolute necessity to link the project to a recognised need in the local community;
- the project must be backed by a professional approach, and the school must ensure that resources, especially time, are available to see through each stage of the scheme;
- the strategy and timing of the project need to be correct and well thought through;
- projects should show vision, innovation, originality and a good dose of lateral thinking;
- schools who have been successful have been determined, patient and persistent, and have not been afraid to learn from their mistakes.

Appendix 1
Contact details

Throughout the guide there are references to the many agencies that are now involved in education fund-raising. Many of these are specifically detailed in Chapter 4, and contact details of these organisations are as follows.

The Specialist Schools Programme

Based at the DfEE at Sanctuary Buildings,
Great Smith Street,
London SW1P 3BT
Tel: 0207 925 5000
Fax: 0207 925 6000
Public enquiries: 0207 925 5555
Website: www.dfee.gov.uk/specschl

Technology Colleges Team

Tel: 0207 925 5837/5838/5833/5419/5400

Language College Team

Tel: 0207 925 5807/6109

Sports and Arts Colleges Team

Tel: 0207 925 5484/5884/5622

Specialist Schools Unit

Fax: 0207 925 6374

Technology Colleges (TC) Trust

23rd Floor,
Millbank Tower (West),
London SW1P 4QP
Tel: 0207 802 2300
Fax: 0207 802 2345

External Relations/Sponsorship

37, Queen's Gate,
London SW7 5HR
Tel: 0207 581 7393
Fax: 0207 581 7388

Youth Sport Trust

3rd Floor,
Woburn Building,
1–7, Woburn Walk,
London WC1H 0JJ
Tel: 0207 388 4436
Fax: 0207 388 4434

Public Private Partnership (PPP) Projects for Schools

The Schools Private Finance team are based at Area 3E of the
Sanctuary Buildings address of the DfEE.
Tel: 0207 925 5262
Fax: 0207 925 6987
Website: www.dfee.gov.uk

Public Private Partnerships Programme (4Ps)

The Local Government Association,
35, Great Smith Street,
London SW1P 3BJ
Tel: 0207 664 314

The New Deal for Schools (NDS) Initiative

The NDS Team are also based at the Sanctuary Buildings address of the DfEE. Contact can be made either through the enquiries number or their website: www.dfee.gov.uk/newdeal.

The National Lottery

The best way to gain information on the National Lottery, especially on contact details, application forms and guidance information, is through the Internet websites:

National Lottery: www.lottery.culture.gov.uk
Sports Lottery bids: www.english.sports.org.uk
Arts Lottery bids: www.artscouncil.org.uk
New Opportunities Fund: www.nof.org.uk

The following contact numbers are also useful:

Arts

Arts Council of England: 0207 312 0123
Scottish Arts Council: 0131 226 6051
Arts Council of Northern Ireland: 01232 667 000
Arts Council of Wales: 01222 388 288

Awards for All

England: 0845 600 2040
Scotland: 0645 700 777

Department for Culture, Media and Sport

Tel: 0207 211 6200

Heritage Lottery Fund

Tel: 0207 591 6041/2/3

The Millennium Commission

Tel: 0207 880 2030

National Lottery Charities Board

Application forms: 0345 919 191
General enquiries: 0207 747 5299

New Opportunities Fund

General enquiries: 0845 0000 120
England: 0845 0000 121
Wales: 0845 0000 122
Scotland: 0845 0000 123
Northern Ireland: 0845 0000 124

Sports

English Sports Council: 0345 649 649
Scottish Sports Council: 0131 339 9000
Sports Council for Northern Ireland: 01232 382 222
Sports Council for Wales: 01222 397 571

European funding initiatives

For a list of all MEPs and their addresses contact:

The European Parliament,
London Office
Tel: 0207 227 4300

The European Commission is based at:

>Rue de la Loi 200,
>B-1049 Brussels,
>Belgium

Or contact the London Office:

>Tel: 0207 973 1992
>Fax: 0207 973 1900/1910

Department of Trade and Industry (DTI)

>Education and Training Branch,
>Kingsgate House,
>68–74 Victoria Street,
>London SW1E 6SW
>Tel: 0207 215 2859
>Website: www.dti.gov.uk

The Socrates Series is managed by:

>The Central Bureau for Educational Visits and Exchanges,
>10, Spring Gardens,
>London SW1A 2BN
>Tel: 0207 389 4157
>Fax: 0207 389 4426
>e-mail: socrates@centralbureau.org.uk
>Website: europa.eu.int/en/xomm/dg22/socrates

Eurodesk is based at the Youth Exchange Centre at the Central Bureau for Educational Visits and Exchanges.

Tel: 0207 389 4033

The British Section of the Franco-British Council is at:

47/49 Strutton Ground,
London SW1P 2HY
Tel: 0207 976 8380
Fax: 0207 976 8131

Contacts relating to Landfill tax schemes

ENTRUST

154, Buckingham Palace Road,
London SW1W 9TR
Tel: 0207 823 4574

The Landfill Tax help desk

c/o HM Customs and Excise
Tel: 0645 128484

Grant-Awarding Trusts

The ADAPT Trust

8, Hampton Terrace,
Edinburgh
Tel: 0131 346 1999

BBC Children in Need

Administration Unit,
PO Box 7,
London W12 8UD
Tel: 0208 735 5057
Fax: 0208 576 8887

Calouste Gulbenkian Foundation

98, Portland Place,
London W1N 4ET
Tel: 0207 636 5313
Fax: 0207 637 3421

Sir John Cass's Foundation

31, Jewry Street,
London EC3N 2EY
Tel: 0207 480 5884
Fax: 0207 488 2519

Charity Projects (Comic Relief)

74, New Oxford Street,
London WC1A 1EF
Tel: 0207 820 5555
Fax: 0207 820 5500

Sir Cliff Richard (Charitable Trust) Ltd

Harley House,
94, Hare Lane,
Claygate,
Esher,
Surrey KT10 0RB
Tel: 01372 467 752
Fax: 01372 462 352

The Foundation for Sports and Arts

PO Box 20,
Liverpool L13 1HB
Tel: 0151 259 5505
Fax: 0151 230 0664

The Paul Hamlyn Foundation

Sussex House,
12, Upper Mall,
London W6 9TA
Tel: 0207 227 3500
Fax: 0207 222 0601

The Mackintosh Foundation

Watchmaker Court,
33, St John's Lane,
London EC1M 4DB
Tel: 0207 405 2000
Fax: 0207 814 9421

The Nuffield Foundation

28, Bedford Square,
London WC1B 3EG
Tel: 0207 631 0566
Fax: 0207 323 4877

The Prince's Trust

18, Park Square East,
London NW1 4LH
Tel: 0207 543 1234
Fax: 0207 543 1200

The Wolfson Foundation

8, Queen Anne Street,
London W1M 9LD
Tel: 0207 323 5730
Fax: 0207 323 3241

Commercial Support in Education

Allied Domecq Trust

24, Portland Place,
London W1N 4BB
Tel: 0207 323 9000
Fax: 0207 323 1742

Barclays New Futures Programme (Kellaway Ltd)

2, Portland Road,
Holland Park,
London W11 4LA
Tel: 0207 221 7883
Fax: 0207 229 4595

BT Schools Link/Education Service

PPC8C, BT Centre,
81, Newgate Street,
London EC1A 7AJ
Tel: 0800 800 848

ICI/Dulux

Community Projects Office,
PO Box 343,
London WC2E 8RJ
Tel: 01753 550000
Fax: 0208 998 3065

Kodak Education Services

Tel: 01442 845169
Fax: 01442 845180

Lloyds/TSB Foundation

PO Box 140,
St Mary's Court,
20 St Mary at Hill,
London EC3R 8NA
Tel: 0207 204 5276
Fax: 0207 204 5275

Ronald McDonald Children's Charities

11–59, High Road,
East Finchley,
London N2 8AW
Tel: 0208 700 7187

Save & Prosper Educational Trust

Finsbury Dials,
20, Finsbury Street,
London EC2 9AY
Tel: 0207 417 2332
Fax: 0207 417 2300

National organisations associated with fund-raising

Association for Business Sponsorship of the Arts (ABSA)

Nutmeg House,
60, Gainsford Street,
Butlers Wharf,
London SE1 2NY
Tel: 0207 378 8143
Fax: 0207 407 7527

Association of Fund-raising Consultants

The Grove,
Harpenden,
Herts AL5 1AH
Tel: 01582 762446
Fax: 01582 461489
Website: www.afc.org.uk

Business in the Community

44, Baker Street,
London W1M 1DH
Tel: 0207 224 1600
Fax: 0207 486 1700

Charities Aid Foundation

Kings Hill,
West Malling,
Kent ME19 4TA
Tel: 01732 520000
Fax: 01732 520001

The Charities Commission

London Office,
Harmsworth House,
13–15, Bouverie Street,
London EC4Y 8DP
Fax: 0171 674 2300

Liverpool Office,
29, Kings Parade,
Queens Dock,
Liverpool L3 4DQ
Fax: 0151 703 1555

Taunton Office,
Tangier,
Taunton,
Somerset TA1 4BL
Fax: 01823 345003

General enquiries: 0870 333 0123
Website: www.charity-commission.gov.uk

CSV (Community Service Volunteers)

237, Pentonville Road,
London N1 9NJ
Tel: 0207 278 6601
Fax: 0207 713 0560

The Directory of Social Change

24, Stephenson Way,
London NW1 2DP
Tel: 0207 209 0902
Fax: 0207 209 5049

Institute of Charity Fund-raising Managers

1, Nine Elms Lane,
London SW8 5NQ
Tel: 0207 627 3436
Fax: 0207 627 3508

National Consumer Council

Consumer Support Department
20, Grosvenor Gardens,
London SW1W 0DH
Tel: 0207 730 3469
Fax: 0207 730 0191

National Council for Voluntary Organisations

Regent's Wharf,
8, All Saints Street,
London N1 9RL
Tel: 0207 713 6161
Fax: 0207 713 6300

Society of Educational Consultants

Enquiries Officer,
256, Longfellow Road,
Coventry CV2 5HJ
Tel: 01203 442 701

Appendix 2

Recommended reading

Many of the case studies in this guide are similar to those published in a monthly journal *Schools Funding Update*, a monthly bulletin on income generation for schools, published by:

Pearson Publishing,
128, Long Acre,
London WC2E 9AN
Subscriptions Tel: 01795 414884
Fax: 01795 414555
Editorial Tel: 01926 452575

The Education Funding Guide: Support from Government Trusts and Companies is published by the Directory of Social Change, and edited by Susan Forrester, Anne Mountfield and Alka Patel.

The Educational Grants Directory, by John Smyth and Kate Wallace, is published by the Directory of Social Change.

European Funding Guide for Schools – published by the Community Education Development Centre, in conjunction with the DfEE, is available from:

CEDC,
Woodway Park School,
Wigston Road,
Coventry CV2 2R
Tel: 01203 655700
Fax: 0247 6655701

School Fund-raising – What You Need to Know, written by Anne Mountfield, is now in its second edition and is published by the Directory of Social Change.

Causes for Courses – A Guide to Classroom Resources from Voluntary Organisations is written by Susan Forrester and published by the Directory of Social Change.

From time to time there are articles relating to fund-raising in education or resource issues printed in the Education Sections of the *Guardian* or the *Independent* newspapers, together with *The Times Educational Supplement.*

Publications dealing with Trusts and Foundations

The Directory of Grant Making Trusts 1997–98 is published by the Charities Aid Foundation.

A Guide to Major Trusts, by Paul Brown and David Casson and published by the Directory of Social Change, comes in two volumes – the first dealing with the top 300 Trusts and the second with 700 further Trusts.

A Guide to Local Trusts is also written by Paul Brown and David Casson, is published by the Directory of Social Change, and comes in four volumes covering the geographical areas of London, the Midlands, the North of England, and the South of England.

Baring Asset Management Top 3000 Charities for 1999 is published by Caritas Data at:

Kemp House,
152–160, City Road,
London EC1V 2NP
Tel: 0171 250 1777
Fax: 0171 250 3050

How to: Apply to a Grant Making Trust is written by Anne Villemur and published by the Charities Aid Foundation.

Publications dealing with commercial support in education

A Guide to Company Giving 1997/98 by Paul Brown and John Smyth is published by the Directory of Social Change.

Building Effective School-Business Links is published by:

Westex Publications Centre,
PO Box 2193,
London E15 2EU
Tel: 0181 533 2000

The 1999 Examples of Excellence and *Partnership Points – The Education Business Partnership Newsletter* are published by:

Business in the Community,
44, Baker Street,
London W1M 1DH
Tel: 0171 224 1600
Fax: 0171 486 1700
Website: www.bitc.org.uk

Sponsorship in Schools – Good Practice Guidelines is a brochure published by:

The National Consumer Council,
20 Grosvenor Gardens,
London SW1W 0DH
Tel: 0171 730 3469
Fax: 0171 730 0191

Working with Education is a document published by BT and available from:

BT Schools Link,
BT Education Service,
81, Newgate Street,
London EC1A 7AJ
Tel: 0800 800 848

Website: www.bt.com

Support for Schools: A Guide for Employers is still available from the DfEE Publications Office, as is documentation relating to the Specialist Schools Initiative.

DfEE Publications,
PO Box 5050,
Sudbury,
Suffolk CO10 6ZQ
Tel: 0845 6022260
Website: www.dfee.gov.uk

Publications dealing with project management

The Complete Guide to Creating and Managing New Projects for Charitable and Voluntary Organisations is written by Alan Lawrie and is published by the Directory of Social Change.

Capital Fund-raising for Schools is written by Sue Marsden and is published by Pitman Publishing.

Publications dealing with fund-raising events

Good Ideas for Raising Serious Money – Large Scale Event Plans and *Tried and Tested Ideas for Raising Money Locally – Small and Medium Scale Events* are both written by Sarah Passingham and published by the Directory of Social Change.

Publications relating to the legal aspects of fund-raising

Starting a Charity is a leaflet published by:

The Charity Commission,
Harmsworth House,
13–15 Bouverie Street,

London EC4Y 8DP
Tel: 0870 333 0123
Publications voicemail: 01823 345427
Website: www.charity-commission.gov.uk

Charitable Status: A Practical Handbook written by Andrew
Phillips and published by the Directory of Social Change.

Appendix 3

Top 100 National Lottery awards to schools and colleges, 1995–99

School/college	Amount	Date	*	LEA
1 Moseley School	4,042,649	12/12/96	H/S	Birmingham
2 The Dormston School	3,940,295	7/23/96	A/S	Dudley
3 John Warner School	3,924,506	4/15/99	S	Broxbourne
4 Hackney Community College	3,129,000	10/10/96	S	Hackney
5 Canterbury High School	3,008,822	3/4/99	S	Canterbury
6 Bognor Regis Community College	2,231,634	4/9/98	S	Arun
7 Barking Abbey School	2,132,881	4/9/98	S	Barking/ Dagenham
8 Trinity C of E High School	1,998,887	6/26/97	S	Manchester
9 Ormesby School	1,938,958	7/8/98	S	Middles- brough
10 St Luke's School	1,726,100	12/8/98	S	Portsmouth
11 Dartford Grammar School	1,671,350	3/18/98	A	Dartford
12 Small Heath GM School	1,605,083	2/5/97	S	Birmingham
13 The Winston Churchill School	1,572,625	5/14/99	S	Woking
14 Millbrook School	1,537,545	5/23/97	S	Southampton
15 Bournemouth School	1,441,142	12/10/98	S	Bournemouth
16 Estover Community College	1,295,000	2/21/96	A	Plymouth

School/college	Amount	Date	*	LEA
17 Bethnal Green High School	1,231,313	7/22/98	S	Tower Hamlets
18 Latimer School	1,222,125	5/13/97	A	Kettering
19 Wyvern School	1,204,550	8/8/97	S	North Somerset
20 Fowey Community School	1,190,339	10/7/98	S	Cornwall
21 Cardinal Heenan High School	1,173,029	6/4/98	S	Liverpool
22 Sandown Court Community College	1,060,000	1/29/99	S	Tunbridge Wells
23 Parmiter's School	1,051,000	6/18/96	S	Three Rivers
24 Fulbrook School	1,038,800	3/20/97	S	Runnymede
25 Dean Close School	1,000,000	3/24/97	A	Cheltenham
26 Haybridge High School	866,526	9/30/96	S	Hereford/ Worcester
27 Kings' School	858,762	5/20/98	S	Hampshire
28 George Abbot School	836,485	1/9/96	S	Surrey
29 Portslade Community College	825,254	5/16/97	S	Brighton & Hove
30 Sir John Talbot School	774,326	7/21/98	S	Shropshire
31 Francis Bacon School	762,500	6/24/98	S	St Albans
32 Newent Community School	738,723	5/14/97	S	Forest of Dean
33 Arthur Terry School	732,965	6/14/95	S	Birmingham
34 Malory School	725,500	1/31/96	S	Lewisham
35 The Magna Carta School	725,000	2/21/96	A	Runnymede
36 Withywood School	716,897	7/9/97	S	Bristol
37 Roade School	683,015	7/9/99	S	Northants
38 Shoeburyness School	680,509	11/25/96	S	Essex
39 The Burton Borough School	676,000	7/16/97	A	Shropshire
40 Keswick School	671,000	6/20/96	S	Allerdale
41 Uplands Community College	653,354	3/5/96	S	East Sussex
42 Burleigh Community College	649,520	10/24/97	S	Charnwood

School/college	Amount	Date	*	LEA
43 Cranford Community College	640,991	1/8/97	S	Hounslow
44 The Matthew Arnold School	614,810	11/25/96	S	Surrey
45 Castle School	611,000	8/20/96	S	Somerset
46 Moulton School	587,689	9/2/97	S	Northants
47 Cape Cornwall Community School	578,473	8/18/98	S	Cornwall
48 Almondbury High School	578,000	10/25/96	S	Kirklees
49 Weston Favell Upper School	553,750	8/8/95	S	Northampton
50 Great Sankey County High School	550,329	10/5/98	S	Warrington
51 Bishop Stopford School	549,436	8/11/97	S	Kettering
52 Huntington School	539,542	2/2/99	S	York
53 Prince Henry's High School	538,950	6/6/95	S	Hereford/ Worcester
54 East Bergholt High School	525,024	11/7/95	S	Suffolk
55 St Aidans County High School	522,346	9/26/97	S	Carlisle
56 Rhyn Park School	520,625	6/26/96	A	Oswestry
57 The Holywood Rudolf Steiner School	508,695	6/4/99	C	North Down
58 Rees Thomas School	505,800	7/11/95	S	Cambridge- shire
59 St Aubyn's School	503,190	4/7/96	S	Waltham Forest
60 Bainacraig School Trust	500,000	06/17/99	C	Perth & Kinross
61 Archway School	497,000	10/10/96	S	Gloucester- shire
62 Sir Charles Lucas School	477,781	10/8/96	S	Colchester
63 Howard Of Effingham School	472,000	6/10/96	S	Surrey
64 Stanney County High School	469,377	5/10/96	S	Cheshire

School/college	Amount	Date	*	LEA
65 Alumwell School Community Association	466,029	6/24/96	S	Walsall
66 Bohunt Community School	461,136	12/16/98	S	East Hampshire
67 Burnt Mill School	447,924	6/23/98	S	Essex
68 Murray Park Community School	437,798	3/20/97	A	Derby
69 Cullomptton Community College	433,070	9/29/97	S	Devon
70 Langley Secondary School	431,782	5/13/97	A	Solihull
71 Heathfield School	428,070	7/20/96	S	Cheshire
72 The Laurel Park School Co Ltd	423,208	5/28/97	S	Glasgow
73 King Edward VII Upper School	417,558	5/16/95	S	Melton
74 The Glasgow High School Club Ltd	401,158	8/28/96	S	Glasgow
75 Willows High School	401,149	7/12/96	A	Cardiff
76 Sir Thomas Rich's School	400,000	11/20/97	S	Gloucester-shire
77 Thornton Grammar School	386,909	9/8/98	S	Bradford
78 Lawrence Sheriff School	384,500	9/5/95	S	Rugby
79 The Mountbatten School	380,437	2/21/96	A	Test Valley
80 Crawshaw School	377,613	8/6/98	S	Leeds
81 The Hedley Walter School Sports Trust	369,204	9/3/97	S	Brentwood
82 Mill Chase School	364,533	12/2/97	S	Hampshire
83 Burgate School	363,585	1/20/98	S	New Forest
84 Wigan Deanery C of E High School	361,727	7/9/97	S	Wigan
85 Watford Grammar School For Boys	345,611	6/3/97	S	Watford
86 Henry Cort School	340,000	4/16/98	S	Hampshire
87 William Parker School	339,368	3/5/97	S	East Sussex

School/college	Amount	Date	*	LEA
Hipperholme and Lightcliffe High School	332,500	2/5/97	S	Calderdale
89 Rainham School for Girls	331,240	10/7/96	S	Medway
90 Godmanchester Primary School	328,000	3/24/98	S	Cambridgeshire
91 Beaconsfield High School	322,200	5/16/95	S	South Bucks
92 Llanfyllin High School	318,970	3/21/97	A	Powys
93 Lady Lumley's School	317,500	4/14/99	S	North Yorkshire
94 Old Grammar School Trust	312,200	7/31/97	H	Rochdale
95 Pindar School	310,000	5/11/98	S	North Yorkshire
96 Lytham St Annes High School	304,996	1/9/96	S	Lancashire
97 Neale-Wade Community College	302,760	5/18/98	S	Cambridgeshire
98 Goffs School	291,905	3/20/97	S	Broxbourne
99 Deanes School	291,717	4/24/96	S	Castle Point
100 Warren School	291,388	4/23/97	S	Barking/ Dagenham

Notes:
S denotes Sport Council
A denotes Arts Council
H denotes Heritage Lottery Fund
C denotes National Lottery Charities Board

Index

CAN ALTERNATIVE SOURCES OF FUNDING BRING YOUR SCHOOL
COMMERCIAL SUPPORT, COMMUNITY AWARENESS AND RAISE
EDUCATIONAL STANDARDS?

Government funding for education is limited and schools are increasingly
having to raise funds through schemes involving community and
commercial support. The OFSTED inspection programme expects schools
to produce detailed management plans including how they will find the
resources to realise these plans.

This practical guide explains everything that schools need to know about
funding, including:

- who to involve in fund-raising
- where to look for sources of funding
- how to set and meet fund-raising targets
- case studies of fund-raising initiatives
- contact details of useful organisations.

All schools looking to develop commercial and community partnerships
should invest in a copy of this guide: the answer to every headteacher's
funding prayer.

PAUL MORRIS has substantial experience of financial management in an
education setting and runs his own Educational Resource Improvement
Consultancy (ERIC).

EDUCATION MANAGEMENT

Cover Design Egelnick+Webb

ISBN 0-415-22957-X

9 780415 229579

ROUTLEDGE FALMER
Taylor & Francis Group

11 New Fetter Lane, London EC4P 4EE
29 West 35th Street, New York NY 10001
www.routledgefalmer.com Printed in GB